Leadership
for School Improvement
in the Caribbean

Editor:
Austin Ezenne

INFORMATION AGE PUBLISHING, INC.
Charlotte, NC • www.infoagepub.com

First published in 2008 by the Department of Educational Studies,
University of the West Indies, Kingston, Jamaica

ISBN: 978-1-60752-370-3 (pbk.)
    978-1-60752-371-0 (e-book)

Printed in the United States of America

CONTENTS

INTRODUCTION *(vi)*
> *Beverley Bryan*
> HOD of Education and Director, School of Education, University of the West Indies, Kingston, Jamaica.

FOREWORD *(ix)*
> *Zellynne Jennings*
> HOD of Education 2001 to 2006 and Director, School of Education 2002 to 2006, University of the West Indies, Kingston, Jamaica.

EDITORIAL *(xiii)*
> *Austin Ezenne*
> Department of Educational Studies, University of the West Indies, Mona, Jamaica.

CONTRIBUTING AUTHORS *(xvii)*

EDITORIAL CONSULTANTS *(xix)*

SECTION 1
SCHOOL EFFECTIVENESS
AND DISCIPLINE

CHAPTER 1.
> *Pages 3 - 32*
> Characteristics of an Effective School:
> A theoretical Perspective.
> *Loraine D. Cook*
> Department of Educational Studies, University of the West Indies, Mona, Jamaica.

CHAPTER 2.
> *Pages 33 - 56*
> Improving Classroom Management and Discipline through the use of, non-verbal Language Techniques.
> *Susan Anderson*
> Department of Educational Studies, University of the West Indies, Mona, Jamaica.

CHAPTER 3.

Pages 57 - 78
School Leadership, Partnerships, Discipline and Student
Outcomes in an Urban Elementary School:
Notes from the Field
Miles Anthony Irving
College of Education, Georgia State University, Atlanta
Georgia. U.S.A.

SECTION 2.
EVALUATION OF
EDUCATIONAL POLICIES

CHAPTER 4.

Pages 81 - 108
Instructional Language Policies for Creolese Speakers in
Guyana: Examining their Social and Academic Outcomes
using Comparative Examples from Eight Countries.
Béatrice Boufoy-Bastick
Department of Liberal Arts, French Section,
University of the West Indies,
St. Augustine, Trinidad & Tobago.

CHAPTER 5.

Pages 109 - 142
Policy implications of project evaluation in Guyana:
The case of the Secondary School Reform Project.
Claudette Phoenix
Measurement and Evaluation Unit, National Centre for
Educational Resource Development, Ministry of
Education, Georgetown, Guyana.

CHAPTER 6.

Pages 143 - 178
Rethinking the Financing of the Education System in
Jamaica.
Disraeli M. Hutton
Department of Educational Studies, University of the
West Indies, Mona, Jamaica.

SECTION 3.
SCHOOL IMPROVEMENT

CHAPTER 7.

Pages 181 - 212

Principals' and Teachers' Perceptions of Principals' Instructional Leadership Roles in Selected Primary Schools in Central Jamaica

Beverley Johnson

Principal, Jericho Primary School, St. Catherine, Jamaica.

& Austin Ezenne

Department of Educational Studies, University of the West Indies, Mona, Jamaica.

CHAPTER 8.

Pages 213 - 246

Secondary School Principals' Perceptions of the Management and Curricular Roles of Librarians in Jamaican Schools

Myrtle Elaine Harris

Documentation Centre, School of Education, University of the West Indies, Mona, Jamaica.

CHAPTER 9.

Pages 247 - 268

Teachers' and Students' Perceptions of Vocational and Technical Education Programme Planning in Jamaican High Schools.

Earl Christian

Ministry of Education and Culture, Kingston, Jamaica

& Austin Ezenne

Department of Educational Studies, University of the West Indies, Mona, Jamaica.

CHAPTER 10.

Pages 269 - 294

Charting the Education Transformation Path: Towards Models of Praxis for Teacher Development for School Improvement in Jamaica

Paulette Feraria

Department of Educational Studies, University of the West Indies, Mona, Jamaica.

NOTES ON CONTRIBUTORS.

Pages 295 - 299

INTRODUCTION

BEVERLEY BRYAN PH.D
HOD of Education and Director, School of
Education, University of the West Indies,
Kingston, Jamaica.

This is a timely and important book. The Caribbean has for some time been pre-occupied with educational transformation, with how to inculcate lasting and affective change in those individuals who will form the leadership and make a difference in the education system as a whole. The people so charged are principals and other institution builders. The contents of the book demonstrate that the process of change for development can happen at different levels in different ways and will involve different areas of expertise and research. Therefore, what we have in this book are researchers who are exploring these varied ways in which we can move toward fundamental and integrative change.

The book, therefore, deals in detail with issues of leadership. At the theoretical level there is exploration of appropriate models of leadership in the effort to create effective schools. At the practical level the importance of the principal's role is explored, especially the individual's own perception of that role in instructional leadership. However, leadership does not simply rest within the school or in one figure. This book explores the range of support mechanisms that need to be in place. Ministries of Education need to provide policy direction on matters such as language education policy which is a critical site of contestation in the Caribbean. Another critical area for development is the technical and vocational curriculum, where the innovative route proposed would include a greater input from teachers in planning the programmes and, therefore, in promoting greater ownership. Individual teachers are, therefore, seen as important agents of change and part of the leadership. However, another contribution to the book suggests that teachers can only achieve that potential and close the transformation gap if the model of teacher development used focuses on self evaluation within a context of school improvement.

The variety of useful and relevant topics is noted in the attention to the critical contextual issue discipline and violence in schools. New solutions for classroom practitioners are proposed in one contribution, whilst another contributor examines an external professional intervention based on community partnerships. This again is timely as there is serious concern about levels of violence encountered in schools and society. Additionally, different sectors are also examined and the case made for a more thorough going reform of secondary education and the targeted financing of the tertiary system.

In the end, it is hoped that readers will take from the articles and chapters ideas about how they can make their institutions more effective learning environments. This should ensure that the book's timeliness is rewarded and that the ideas explored here are carried forward to the people and places where school leadership matters.

FOREWORD

PROFESSOR ZELLYNNE JENNINGS
HOD of Education 2001 to 2006 and
Director, School of Education 2002 to 2006,
University of the West Indies, Kingston,
Jamaica.

Throughout history societies have had enormous expectations of their education systems and particularly of the teachers and principals in the schools. Today is no different. For example, the Task Force on Educational Reform in Jamaica was commissioned to prepare an action plan 'consistent with a vision for the creation of world-class education system that will generate the human capital and produce the skills necessary for Jamaican citizens to compete in the global economy'[1].One of the chapters in this book proposes that the path to transforming education in Jamaica must begin with teachers; they need to re-visit their teaching and "reposition the teacher-self as an agent of change". Another examines the characteristics of an effective school and concludes that at its core is an effective leader. Indeed, a theme underlying most of the chapters is that school improvement depends to a large extent on the quality of leadership offered by principals. They must be good instructional supervisors, but it is not sufficient that they think they are performing that role, the teachers must see them as so doing. This is clear in one chapter in which the authors noted the discrepancies between principals' and teachers' perceptions of the principal as instructional supervisor.

Nearly four decades ago, Seymour Sarason[2] made a point which, no doubt, has been repeated numerous times since, that "any proposal for change that intends to alter the quality of life in the school depends primarily on the principal". While this is so leadership for school improvement cannot rest entirely on the shoulders of the principal. Indeed this seems to be acknowledged in discussions on transformational leadership. Leithwood and Jantzi[3] emphasize that authority and influence associated with this form of leadership are not necessarily allocated to those occupying formal administrative positions but "power is attributed by organizational members to whomever is able to inspire their commitments to collective aspirations and the desire for personal and collective mastery over the capacities needed to accomplish such aspirations" (p204). That transformational leadership becomes the collective responsibility of leaders in an organization becomes evident on closer examination of what that form of leadership entails. To Leithwood and Jantzi it involves three broad categories of practices: (i) setting directions: (ii) developing people and : (iii) redesigning the organization. The first includes building a 'school vision', setting goals and priorities and having high performance expectations. The second involves providing intellectual stimulation, offering individualized support and modelling desirable professional practices and values. The third category includes the development of a collaborative school culture, enabling participation in decision making and developing supportive community relationships. Vice principals of schools, senior teachers, heads of departments, school librarians then are among the school leaders who all have a role to play. Likewise partners of the school. Partnership is the focus of one of the chapters which deals with the collaboration between an urban elementary school principal and a university faculty in an intervention which yielded positive results including improvement in discipline. Another chapter emphasises participation in decision-making and underscores the need for greater opportunities for teachers to participate in the planning of technical –vocational programmes.

The chapters in this book should stimulate the reader not only to think about the kind of leadership that is needed to improve schools in the Caribbean (using 'schools' in the widest sense to range from early childhood to higher education institutions) but also other forms of support. In one chapter it is argued that since Jamaica is on the path to transforming public education, the government needs to pursue a more holistic approach to financing education and target definite areas for funding in higher education; for example the renovation of the physical plant, and upgrading technical and scientific facilities for research.

Two chapters in the book focus on Guyana. One examines language policies which is particularly pertinent in a context where the government should be making provisions for its indigenous population which has some nine different languages. Should a language policy in Guyana not take these into consideration? The second chapter is concerned with the

Secondary School Reform Project which shares in common with Jamaica's Reform of Secondary Education goals of access, quality and equity.

This book is very timely and should prove informative not only to current and prospective leaders but also to students and scholars both locally and internationally with an interest in Caribbean education. The chapters are written in a sufficiently user friendly style to be of interest also to the general public who want to see the process of transformation realised in our education systems.

NOTES

i.   Task Force on Educational Reform Final Report (2004), p.5.

ii. Sarason, S.B. (1971). *The Culture of the School and the Problem of Change* Boston: Allyn & Bacon, p.148.

iii. Leithwood, K., & Jantzi, D. (2006). Transformational school leadership for large-scale reform: effects on students, teachers, and their classroom practices. *School Effectiveness and School Improvement.* Vol 17,No .2: 201-227.

iv   Stenhouse, L. (1993). The teacher as research. Hammersley, M (Ed). *Controversies in Classroom Research.* Buckingham, Open University Press: 223-234.

EDITORIAL NOTE AND ACKNOWLEDGMENT

AUSTIN EZENNE
Department of Educational studies,
University of the West Indies, Jamaica

The diversity of school environments makes 'School Improvement' an ambiguous and problematic term (Seashore-Louis, Toole, & Hargreaves, 1999, p. 251). One of the main contributing factors, as recognised by Dimmock (2002), is that "each school is a unique mix of students and contextual situations" (p.141). Nowhere is this diversity of school location, level, type, demographics, programmes, teachers and students as diverse as here in the Caribbean. It is a consequence that our rich diversity and rapid change pose unique and extreme challenges to leadership for school improvement in the Caribbean (Down, & Nurse, 2007; Rodriguez Gallar, 2007). This volume addresses these challenges.

The peer-reviewed research presented in this volume identifies three categories of systemic issues that currently need our immediate attention as educators, policy-makers and educational administrators. These three categories, corresponding to the three sections of this volume, are:

1. Shaping school leadership, class management and student discipline for school effectiveness
2. Applying sound financial and evaluation directed policy to education for regional development, and

3. Enhancing expectations of Principals, Teachers and Students for optimal school improvement

The authors of this anthology have risen to the challenges, have identified key issues facing current practices and needed reforms, have presented us with empirically supported theoretical analyses and practical solutions in each of these three categories. The papers presented here identify elements of our diversity that call for our immediate attention. However, they also celebrate other aspects of our diversity which our authors identify as the most probable paths to school improvement in the Caribbean.

This volume has been written for our Education students, researchers, school librarians, psychologists and counsellors, for our teachers and Principals, for our Educational Administrators and national policy-makers, who will recognise within these pages those very same issues they face on a day-to-day basis. Hopefully these, our education stakeholders, will also find within these same pages alternative paths and bridges to the successful and permanent resolution of these key educational issues.

I gratefully acknowledge the expertise and dedication of our editorial consultants who have given so much of their time to review the many research papers presented to them and to thank them for the encouragement they have given to our selected authors

EDITORIAL CONSULTANTS

We are grateful to our editorial consultants for their immeasurable contributions to this book on leadership for school improvement. Their contributions, insights and suggestions have added greatly to the quality of the book and we thank them most sincerely.

PROFESSOR ZARIF BACILIOUS

Department of Educational Administration St. John's University, New York, U.S.A

DR. GLORIA BURKE

Department of Educational Studies, The University of the West Indies, Kingston, Jamaica.

PROFESSOR ZELLYNNE JENNINGS-CRAIG

Department of Educational Studies, The University of the West Indies, Kingston Jamaica.

DR. MORRIS HALDEN

Institute of Education, The University of the West Indies, Kingston, Jamaica.

PROFESSOR PHILO HUTCHESON
College of Education, Georgia State:
University, Atlanta, Georgia.

DR. BARBARA MATALON
Institute of Education, The University of
the West Indies, Kingston, Jamaica.

DR. MILES ANTHONY IRVING
College of Education, Georgia State
University, Atlanta, Georgia, U.S.A

PROFESSOR JOHN C.S. MUSAAZI
East African Institute for Higher
Educational Studies and Development
Makerere University, Kampala, Uganda.

and mission statement. This culture also involves a sense of collegiality, which binds together the team of teachers working in the school. The student culture is characterized by individual learning and co-operative learning where help may be obtained from other students or teachers and where team learning takes place (Durian & Butler, 1987).

The question of school effectiveness means different things to different people. Effectiveness can be judged in two ways: a) assessment of outcomes and b) appraisal about certain admirable qualities. Multiple stakeholders play critical roles in defining criteria for effectiveness. There are certain stakeholders who want school to be a place where children learn positive democratic values, citizenship, and discipline (Durian & Butler, 1987). Others see an effective school as one that experiences success not only academically, but also in extra curricula activities such as art shows, musical performances, science fairs and athletic events.

In a meta-analyses, to determine the factors of school effectiveness, Scheerens and Bosker (1997, cited in Scheerens, 1999) analysed and expanded on the meaning of the factors used in ten studies on school effectiveness.

Scheerens and Bosker (1997) used actual questionnaires and scales as data collection instruments to generate suggested factors that could be used as criteria to determine an effective school (see Table 1).

7

Table 1: The Summary Table of Factors and Components in the Scheerens and Bosker (1997) Study

Factors	Components
Achievement orientation, high expectations	• clear focus on the mastering of basic subjects • high expectations (school level) • high expectations (teacher level) • records on pupils' achievement
Educational leadership	• general leadership skills • school leader as information provider • orchestrator or participative decision making • school leader as coordinator • meta-controller of classroom processes • time educational/administrative leadership • counselor and quality controller of classroom teachers • initiator and facilitator of staff professionalization
Consensus and cohesion among staff	• types and frequency of meetings and consultations • contents of cooperation • satisfaction about cooperation • importance attributed to cooperation • indicators of successful cooperation
Curriculum quality/ opportunity to learn	• the way curricular priorities are set • choice of methods and text books • application of methods and text books • opportunity to learn • satisfaction with the curriculum
School climate	*a) orderly atmosphere* • the importance given to an orderly climate • rules and regulations • punishment and rewarding • absenteeism and drop out • good conduct and behaviour of pupils • satisfaction with orderly school climate *b) climate in terms of effectiveness orientation and good internal relationships* • priorities in an effectiveness-enhancing school climate • perceptions on effectiveness-enhancing conditions • relationships between pupils • relationships between teacher and pupils • relationships between staff • relationships: the role of the head teacher • engagement of pupils • appraisal of roles and tasks • job appraisal in terms of facilities, conditions of labour, task load and general satisfaction • facilities and building

cont ...

Table 1 continued: The Summary Table of Factors and Components in the Scheerens and Bosker (1997) Study

Factors	Components
Evaluative potential	• evaluation emphasis • monitoring pupils' progress • use of pupil monitoring systems • school process evaluation • use of evaluation results • keeping records on pupils' performance • satisfaction with evaluation activities
Parental involvement	• emphasis on parental involvement in school policy • contacts with parents • satisfaction with parental involvement
Classroom climate	• relationships within the classroom • order • work attitude • satisfaction
Effective learning time	• importance of effective learning • time • monitoring of absenteeism • time at school • time at classroom level • classroom management • homework

Adapted from: Scheerens, 1999

More recently, other researchers have investigated characteristics considered important for an effective school. For example, Lunenburg and Ornstein (2004) using the Connecticut School Effectiveness Project report cited the following seven factors as characteristics of effective schools:

1. A SAFE AND ORDERLY ENVIRONMENT:

An environment that is not repressive and authoritarian. In other words an environment that lends itself to the care and nuturing of students and provides teachers with a sense of support and collegiality. The teachers are protected from hostile and unreasonable outside forces. In Jamaica, for example, the principal in schools are shields between the outside forces and the teacher. If a complaint is levied against a teacher, the principal of the school is responsible for calling a meeting with the complainer and the teacher. In public schools if the principal deems that the case is not trivial, he/she will refer the matter to the school board. Once the complain is submitted to the board in writing, the board refers the matter to a personnel committee which consist of :

- "The chair of the board;
- One government nominee; and
- The representative on the board of the category of accused personnel" (The Education Act, 1980, p.33).

If the teacher disagrees with the decision of the committee the teacher may "appeal to the Appeals Tribunal"(at the Ministry of Education, Youth and Culture). This protective covering is provided to teachers by the government who governs and regulates the school systems through policies and regulations.

2. A CLEAR SCHOOL MISSION:

A school mission that is supported by staff. This mission encompasses instructional goals, assessment procedures and accountability. The priorities of the school are the priorities of its employees. In Jamaica most schools provide teachers upon employment with a

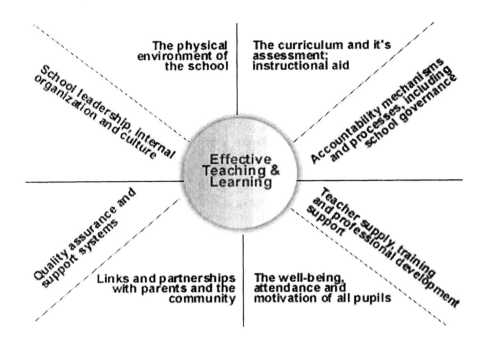

Figure : 1 Examining effective school and teachers by domain
Source: http://www1.worldbank.org/education/est/resources/resource2000.htm

THE CURRICULUM AND ITS ASSESSMENT:

Reviewing and restructuring the curriculum involves standardizing certain content area of the curriculum. The government of Jamaica has stated that it is the responsibility of the state to "develop, implement, monitor and evaluate the education curriculum in keeping with set standards for the first 13 years of the school system" (Education: The way upward, 2001, p.12). In addition the state will provide the necessary educational material to support the curriculum.

ACCOUNTABILITY MECHANISMS AND PROCESSES INCLUDING SCHOOL GOVERNANCE:

Students are to be evaluated and assessed at the school level. The results from these evaluations and assessments should be used to monitor students' achievements and identify those experiencing learning difficulties. The Jamaican government states clearly that teachers are responsible to "consistently assess each student within their care and provide written records of this assessment" (Education: The way upward, 2001, p.12).

TEACHER SUPPLY TRAINING AND PROFESSIONAL DEVELOPMENT SUPPORT:

Effective schools develop statutes to ensure that initial teacher training is administered by accredited institutions. Also ensuring that continued professional training is available to all teachers. While the government of Jamaica holds itself responsible for providing qualified and trained teachers for the schools, the government has also given the teachers college the mandate to provide opportunities for continuous education of teachers. Ten per cent of the staff is allowed to access study leave, with full/ half pay for two years leave. The teachers' training colleges are to research and develop new teaching material and techniques; and to prepare teachers who are academically qualified to teach the required subjects (Education: The way upward, 2001, p.12).

THE WELL-BEING, ATTENDANCE AND MOTIVATION OF ALL PUPILS:

The schools are responsible for monitoring students' attendance. In providing a positive environment teachers are also responsible for influencing the students' motivation. In other words, the school is responsible for helping each child to reach her/his potential. The Jamaican government states that the teachers are to be "caring and responsible towards the students; to provide for the safety and security of the students and to foster the development of the mental and social well being of the student" (Education: the way upward, 2001, p.12).

THE EFFECTIVE SCHOOL DEVELOPS LINKS AND PARTNERSHIPS WITH PARENTS AND THE COMMUNITY:

By entering into a partnership with parents and the community, the schools will be held accountable, less dependent on the government and more integrated with the community. The Jamaican government has stipulated that each parent should be a member of the PTA; the government has also called on the community to support and protect the schools (Education: the way upward, 2001, p.12).

ESTABLISHING QUALITY ASSURANCE SYSTEMS:

This involves regular inspection of the school by independent individuals. In Jamaica the Ministry of Education and culture (MOEC) has decentralize the management and monitoring of the school system by reintroducing Regional offices for ensuring the achievement of educational objectives and targets. The role of the Regional Authorities is limited. The MOEC still retains significant control on critical areas such as financial resources and the hiring of teachers.

THE PHYSICAL ENVIRONMENT OF THE SCHOOL:

This involves the distribution of basic resources into the schools; from safe buildings and sanitation to textbooks and ICT facilities. In Jamaica the state is responsible for providing educational material to support the curriculum for the first 13 years of the school system and the physical infrastructure for schools.

It is important to note that factors of effectiveness generated from studies in developed countries are not always transferable to developing countries. The educational landscape in developing countries is characteristically different. For example, a World Bank report concluded that developing countries place higher priority on increasing primary school enrolment than on children learning adequately (From Schooling Access to Learning Outcomes: An Unfinished Agenda, 2005). Another World Bank report also noted that in some developing countries, schools lacked permanent buildings (Rewrite the Future: Education for Children in Conflict-Affected Countries, 2006). Scheerens (1999) noted that the reviews of studies on educational effectiveness in developing countries show a strong prevalence of the production function type of study.

Leadership within a school is not a permanent position, it is not an inherited status; it is a status obtained by appointment. Coupled with this fact, there are unforeseen circumstances that can result in the removal of a leader. It is therefore imperative that an effective leader develops other leaders and leadership teams within an organization. Fink and Brayman (2006) recommends subsequent to their findings that it should be mandatory for all schools to have a leadership succession plan. The development of leaders should be a shared and distributed responsibility of a leadership team within the school. Fink and Brayman emphasized that leaders in the school communities need autonomy and time to empower others to establish and achieve meaningful school improvement goals. Governments' "standardized and micro- managed reforms" often reduce school leaders to mere functionaries. Even though these micro -managed reforms create short-term improvements, they fail to produce sustainable improvement.

The morale of staff members improves when they are encouraged to participate in decision-making. Also, employees gain the impression that their input is required for the success of the organization; this promotes greater group productivity (Ezenne, 2000). However, having a team that makes decisions for a school is not synonymous with engaging the entire staff in meaningful ways (Cross & Reitzug, 1996). Ingersoll (1996) noted that autonomy and influence over instructional activities will count for little if teachers do not also have power over fundamental socialization and sorting activities.

An effective leader can evaluate and provide for the needs of the task and the environment in which the events are taking place. Somech (2005) investigated the relative effect of a directive leadership approach as compared with a participative leadership approach on school staff teams' motivation. Motivation was determined by staff sense of empowerment and organizational commitment. The results indicated a positive association between directive leadership and organizational commitment. Whereas, there was a positive association between participative leadership and staff-team innovation and empowerment. The researchers concluded that both styles of leadership enhanced school effectiveness and should not be viewed as mutually exclusive, but complimentary.

Even though team building and participatory decision-making is important to the characteristics of effective leadership in the schools, it is equally important that effective leader maintain a psychological distance from their subordinates. According to Handy (1993) a leader "cannot properly control and discipline subordinates if he/she is too close to them emotionally" (p. 104).

In other words, the psychologically distant leader is effective in achieving greater productivity from the group only when the members of the group informally

Peterson, K. D. & Deal, T. E. (1998, September). How leaders Influence the Culture of Schools. *Educational Leadership,* 28 - 30.

Pressley, M., Gaskins, I., Solic, K.,& Collins, S. (2006). A portrait of benchmark school: How a school produces high achievement in students who previously failed. *Journal of Educational Psychology,* 98(2),282-306.

Reynolds, D. (n.d.). Effective school leadership: the contribution of school effectiveness research. Retrieved November 22, 2006, from http://www1.worldbank.org/education/est/resources/topic%20papers/jaap699.doc

Rewrite the future:Education for children in conflict affected country (2005). Retreived November,23,2006, from, http://www.savethechildren.ca/whatwedo/rtf/altpdfs/RewritetheFuture-PolicyReport.pdf

Sanders, L. (2000)What do we know about school effectiveness and improvement. Retrieved November, 22,2006, from, http://www1.worldbank.org/education/est/resources/topic%20papers/Types%20of%20policy.doc

Scheerens J. (1999). School effectiveness in developed and developing countries: a review of the research evidence. Retrieved November 21,2006, from http://www1.worldbank.org/education/est/resources/topic%20papers/jaap699.doc

Somech, A. (2005). Directive versus participative leadership: two complementary approaches to managing school effectiveness. *Educational Administration Quarterly,41(5),*777-795.

Tomlinson, C. A. (1999). The differentiated classroom: Responding to the needs of all learners. Books.google.com

Witmer, M. (2005). Relationships among transformational leadership, family background, teachers' commitment to change, effective schools' characteristics, and student achievement in California public comprehensive high schools:A structural equation model. Retrieved November,23,2006 from, http://gradworks.umi.com/31/60/3160499.html.

World Bank (n.d.). Resources for effective school and teachers. Retrieved November ,21,2006, from, http://www1.worldbank.org/education/est/resources/resource2000.htm

Chapter 2

IMPROVING CLASSROOM
MANAGEMENT AND DISCIPLINE
THROUGH THE USE OF NON-
VERBAL LANGUAGE
TECHNIQUES

SUSAN ANDERSON

ABSTRACT

In Jamaica today, violence is increasing so rapidly that the breakdown in discipline in our schools, as a result of the general social disintegration, is a serious cause for concern. This breakdown is of concern not only to individual families, but also teachers, administrators and indeed the society at large. The rapid growth in indiscipline in schools over recent times has meant that teachers have to be responsive to new and ever changing approaches to classroom management and ultimately student outcomes. Classroom management is among those key areas that are significant to fostering positive behaviour and is a priority if students are to participate effectively in society. Failure to develop an appreciation for a more disciplined and participatory lifestyle has the capacity to dis-empower a generation of children and the future of our society. This paper was designed to shed light both on ways in which nonverbal communication is used in the classroom generally and how teachers can use positive non-verbal techniques effectively to manage and maintain discipline. These techniques not only lead to better classroom outcomes but could better prepare students for the world of work, starting from job applications and interview practices. In fact, nonverbal communication plays an important part in the hiring interview from the perspectives of both applicant and interviewer (Posthuma, Morgensen, & Campion, 2002).

The writer begins by identifying the benefits of school for children and how these are particularly helpful for the child with problems. A classroom management technique is then explored. The reader is informed about significant socio-emotional as well as educational benefits to be derived from consciously incorporating nonverbal techniques in improving classroom management and especially its role in facilitating workable strategies for stemming the tide of degradation of discipline in our schools, especially secondary level Jamaican schools. Knowledge of effective strategies such as non-verbal techniques; which voluntary or even involuntary behaviours to be avoided; and the possible links between classroom discipline and nonverbal behaviours can all be used as the launching pad for a new and improved way of understanding and ultimately changing the negative approaches used by many educators. This paper found that many students displaying aggressive behaviours, especially those at the secondary level, argue that their hostility toward both classmates and teachers is the results of how they have been "dissed" (disrespected). However, also recognised is the other angle that such "disrespect" is often an assumption on the part of the aggressors. In fact, it is common knowledge that many acts of violence are the result of misinterpreted cues from "bad vibes" (feelings). More importantly, however, is the fact that the negative interpretation of students is derived from non-verbal cues such as, "cold-treatment, "being looked down on", being "ignored" or of teachers having a "low expectation" of them. Implications for the development of attributional understandings of this under-researched topic and for practitioners interested in improving classroom management, which can lead to significant achievement outcomes, are reported.

INTRODUCTION

Our schools, especially High Schools in Jamaica and indeed the wider world, are faced nowadays with a bombardment of requests especially from psychologists, and in particular educational psychologists, to find a panacea for the level of indiscipline as well as violence and aggression by students as perpetrators and victims. While there is the possibility that good school climate still exists, we as educators must find ways of dealing with the current wave of unrest and aggression in these schools if we believe in protecting the future of our people. We need to highlight the positives that do exist and borrow from such climates while finding more workable solutions in order to enhance successful living and academically wholesome achievement. We need to "take back" our homes, our schools and our society. As teachers strive for excellence in their effort to educate the "whole child", there are cases of mal-adaptive behaviour pervading the walls of our educational institutions – indiscipline and even threatening terrorism, constantly rearing its ugly head.

Eugene Howard an earlier authority on school climate and discipline wrote:

> "*Schools with positive climates are places where people care, respect, and trust one another. In such a school, people feel a high sense of pride and ownership which comes from each individual having a role in making the school a better place.............. Schools with a positive climate are characterized by people- centred belief and value systems, procedures, rules, regulations and policies*" (1981, p.8).

The question is how are we to successfully manage this dirge? Several methods and strategies have been offered with, in some cases, very little positive outcomes. Maybe we are missing something, we might add, or maybe we should try something else. In so doing we want to make our institutions ones that endorse Howard's 1981 study. We have to look at what we are doing to discover what is lacking from our best intentions and how we can engage corrective measures. The following scenario presents a typical case in some institutions where there is indiscipline that is not necessarily addressed appropriately.

REFLECTING NON-VERBAL CUES AS A MEANS OF EMPOWERMENT

Here the teacher understands and interprets the students non-verbal messages. For example:

1. *I noticed that when you did...... your face ....*
2. *When you did..... your body.................................*

Additionally, by describing specific observed behaviours, the teacher provides insight to the student about how he/she is "coming across" or being perceived. Such responses are descriptive and non-evaluative which allows for the avoidance of negative effect. They do not include accusations or inferences about the other person's motives, attitudes or personality traits. For example, telling a student that he is bad is accusative rather than descriptive. It is critical, especially for young children, to help them make the distinction between themselves and their action. "Are they as human beings, bad people, or are their actions inappropriate to the situation?" The reflective and effective teacher is one who is skilled at analyzing classroom interactions and is particularly sensitive to what is happening in his/her classroom. It stands to reason, therefore, that the empowered teacher is one that has an accurate understanding of what his/her students are doing and not doing and what they are likely to do. This reflective and subsequently effective teacher is fully cognizant of what is happening in the classroom.

PROXIMITY AS A MEANS OF EMPOWERMENT

The teacher's proximity to students is another factor which can have an effect on student's behaviour. Every student and teacher has a deep rooted and culturally established sense of personal territory. Since most classroom behaviour problems occur furthest from the teacher (Fifer, 1986), moving about becomes an important management technique. In the average classroom, teachers and students are separated by twelve (12) or more feet (Miller, 1986).

SENSITIVITY TO THE VARIOUS SUB-CULTURES AS EMPOWERMENT

Teachers must be aware of non-verbal communication when teaching students from the various sub-cultures and socio-economic backgrounds, as well as, exceptionalities students may have. Here again, the type of communication is important. For instance, a student who is abused at home may misinterpret or dislike being touched. Teachers of a particular High school visited by the researcher stated how important it is for them to be familiar with the verbal and non-verbal language rules and mores of the students in the classroom which, at times, put them at a disadvantage and make them poor communicators with students whose backgrounds and experiences differ from their own. When this happens, communication breaks down between teacher and students, and at times, destroys the professional relationship between the teacher and learner. Teachers need to learn to be more sensitive to students' feelings and situations especially when their lifestyle situations are already abusive and uncaring (Leo-Rhynie 1993; Levy and Chevannes 1996).

WITH-HOLDING RESPONSE AS A MEANS OF EMPOWERMENT

Most of us, especially of the older generation, can attest to the fact that we were brought up on the saying that "he who keeps his mouth (shut) keeps his life". Although the saying is folklore, it was widely used to curb any impulsive desire to give especially unnecessary information for fear of reprisal. Nowadays, it is more commonly used especially in garrison-type communities where "its non-observance" could result in the individual actually losing his/her life. A non-response to a student is also an effective discipline technique to use in certain circumstances. Often it is better to ignore a student's action if a confrontation can be avoided and the offence is not too objectionable to students or teachers. According to Walker and Walker (1991), in situations of potential confrontation, the teacher should attempt to wait out the mood before initiating a direct demand. A student in such a situation is likely to interpret the teacher's comment as provocative especially when it is made in the presence of peers. Defusing anger and keeping impulsive thoughts to oneself are two more virtues associated with silence. When one is angry, feeling sick or likely to be unfair or overreact, it is prudent to keep one's silence rather than react in anger. Students have hard days, too, and often what is said in anger is not meant. Of course, major classroom confrontations should be avoided and dealt with at a time when student and teacher can meet outside of class (Chandler & Dahlquist, 2002). Sometimes, when used instructionally, a teacher's intentional silence, as in the concept of "wait time" already mentioned, can be used to encourage students to think for themselves as well as talk to class-mates for answers and solutions to problems. Here peer mediation is extremely useful.

BOOSTING INTEREST AS A MEANS OF EMPOWERMENT

Interest boosting is a process by which the teacher makes a specific effort to show genuine interest in a student's work at the first sign of boredom or restlessness. One way of doing this is for the teacher to go over to the student, observe his work, praise him for his effort and suggests ways that he can improve without criticizing him. Meeks- Gardner et al (2000) found that rewards for children's work are related to reduced aggression. This method allows the teacher to help the student "stay on task" and prevent inappropriate behaviour. On the other hand, if the teacher humiliates the student for "being off task" or "looking as if he would rather be elsewhere", the student is likely to give over to inappropriate behaviour. The student is best served when the caring teacher, with the appropriate attitude, helps him/her over the hurdle by offering help, not criticism, when he/she is frustrated and not coping with a challenging task. This treatment serves to avert explosion or the desire to give up. In this way, the teacher is allowed to provide assistance before the situation becomes uncontrollable. The teacher can use this method to prevent disruptive behaviour, (Weinstein, 2003)

INTERPERSONAL AND COMMUNICATION SKILLS

Teachers should learn to use the above empowerment skills effectively being cognizant that the application of skills must be used in conjunction with attitudes and feelings. The body language and general non-verbal cues tell the student whether the teacher is caring or not. Assertive behaviour, not be confused with passive or aggressive behaviour, according to Emmer et al (2003), is:

> "the ability to stand up for one's legitimate rights in ways that make it less likely that others will ignore or circumvent them" (p. 146)

These researchers explain that teachers display assertive behaviour in the classroom when they use assertive body language by composing themselves and maintaining a reasonable distance between them while, at the same time, facing the offending student. Maintaining enough distance so as not to appear threatening and matching the facial expression with the content of the message being presented to students constitute authority as well as respect all around. Another aspect of this assertiveness demonstrated by the above illustration is an appropriate tone of voice. A clear and deliberate pitch that is slightly raised from the teacher's normal tone could signal to the offender that the teacher is in charge and should be listened to and obeyed. It is also advised that the teacher must be persistent in order that the student follows through with the appropriate behaviour. The student who witnesses the teacher getting flustered, losing temper or giving up in an effort to maintain discipline, is likely to be reinforced in the negative behaviour. Such lack of control can even foster the development of even greater levels of negative and undisciplined behaviour. The assertive teacher will listen to the student's legitimate explanations while at the same time refusing to be diverted by denials, blame game and arguing. Without using one word, the empowered teacher understands:

"I am fully cognizant that my students read my body language. What I say verbally is strongly reinforced with my body movements and facial expressions. As students read these impressions, they can see that I enjoy teaching this subject, that I accept them and will work with them in the way I non-verbally communicate this to them. As part of my teaching style, I also use gestures so that my enthusiasm is evident. Steady eye-contact with my students is an indication that I monitor what I do with them in my class and read their non-verbal communications to me. When I am teaching, I like to move around the classroom and I will get especially close to each student if he/she is displaying inappropriate behaviour. Let me hasten to say that I do, however, understand and respect your position on things; your background is not an issue to me, neither is the way in which you communicate non-

Chapter 3

SCHOOL LEADERSHIP, PARTNERSHIPS, DISCIPLINE AND STUDENT OUTCOMES IN AN URBAN ELEMENTARY SCHOOL: NOTES FROM THE FIELD

MILES ANTHONY IRVING

ABSTRACT

Given the current political climate of educational accountability teacher education programs and school districts in the United States have come under increased pressure to demonstrate the impact of curriculum and school reform on student learning. One strategy that public schools and teacher training institutions have utilized is the development of University/ School District Partnerships. The present chapter is a reflective account of how urban partnerships are established and maintained with a "ground up" approach. Collaboration between an urban elementary school principal and university faculty member is discussed in the context of effective school leadership, school reform, and the creation of interventions for at risk African American males.

Public Schools have experienced an environment of educational accountability since the implementation of the No Child Left Behind legislation in 2001. The atmosphere of educational accountability has placed teacher education programs and school districts under increased pressure to demonstrate the impact of curriculum and school reform on student learning. One strategy that public schools and teacher training institutions have utilized is the development of University/School District Partnerships. While university and school partnerships have been in place for many decades in the United States, over the last 15 years formal relationships between universities and school districts have increased greatly (Ravid & Handler, 2001).

Proposed sanctions primarily through cuts in funding for public schools designated as low performing and the need for institutions of higher education to document how their teacher education programs improve student learning has spurred the increase in educational partnerships (Mathie, 2002; Sandholtz, 2002). Creating a successful partnership between two large educational systems can be difficult due to the many factors involved (Borthwick, Stirling, Nauman, & Cook, 2003). School districts and Universities operate within very different paradigms. The development a partnership often requires both parties to be responsive to deadlines and initiate change through adopting new strategies and sometimes adjusting policies. Often with the implementation of a university and school district partnership there are several levels of personnel and bureaucratic structure that must also be successfully negotiated before basic decisions can be made. Professional organizations have been created with a focus on partnerships and a dialogue continues to take place across the country (Peel & Peel, 2002). This chapter is a case study that explores themes that emerged during the first years of a partnership with a university and an urban elementary school. This chapter also chronicles the process of how the partnership was used to create an intervention for African American children with a history of behavior problems.

INTRODUCTION

In 2001, the College of Education at Georgia State University and the Atlanta Public Schools began to form a long-term partnership focused on developing, and implementing a comprehensive, collaborative, and proactive response to reform. The efforts to initiate the partnership began with a focus on current challenges, needs and issues facing the Atlanta Public Schools, an urban school district, and Georgia State University as and an urban research university. The Partner Schools Initiative was developed and designed to infuse concentrated efforts from university faculty within designated schools in the district. Several planning and design meetings were held to establish procedures and protocols for the work that would take place under this initiative.

The present chapter is a reflective account of how urban partnerships are established and maintained with a "ground up" approach. Often when new partnerships are formed between major institutions the impetus and framing of the partnership emerges from those in leadership positions. These "top down" approaches experience difficulty when there is a lack of buy in from employees and midlevel administrators. A "ground up" approach is established in schools by involving teachers and school administrators in creation of the rationale, formation, development, and goals of the partnership. The Atlanta Public Schools and Georgia State University used a ground up approach to form and develop a schools partner initiative.

CONCEPTUALIZING AND SELECTING UNIVERSITY URBAN LIAISONS

Georgia State University's College of Education (COE) Urban Partnership Steering Committee, comprised of self-selected department chairs, faculty members, and the associate dean, conceptualized the idea of field-based faculty members that would represent the COE within the designated partner schools. The field-based faculty member positions were titled Urban Liaisons (UL). During the conceptualization stage, the steering committee identified specific characteristics that would be optimal for an effective UL. Five specific UL characteristics were identified by the steering committee including; (a) a commitment to urban education; (b) a commitment to partnerships in urban schools; (c) knowledge of current public school reform initiatives; (d) the ability to work well with faculty, staff, students and parents; (e) professional experience in K-12 classrooms.

A general call for any COE faculty interested in serving as a UL was disseminated. A brief description of the UL role was provided in the announcement with no compensation or course release time initially included. The steering committee purposefully omitted the parameters of compensation to ascertain which faculty members were genuinely interested in the role. Among a faculty of 150 members, a handful of faculty responded to the announcement. The ULs were chosen through an interview process conducted by steering committee.

The primary role of the UL was to broker services for the partner school. That is, if the administrator or a faculty member needed a specific type of support, the UL would try to facilitate support for the need. The duties of the UL included; (a) conducting teacher observations; (b) working with the school-appointed liaison; (c) attending faculty and parent meetings, as appropriate; (d) participating in Urban Partnership Steering Committee meetings; (e) committing a minimum of one day per week at the partner school site. While these were the initial roles and duties, individual ULs have expanded their roles to include participating on the Local School Administrative Council, training teachers in best practices, and conducting research projects at the school level. The author was selected to be the liaison for Connally Elementary school in Atlanta. The remaining part of this chapter will highlight how the partnership was used improve school disciplinary issues by focusing on at risk African American males students with a history of behavior problems.

THE EXPRESS TO SUCCESS: CONNALLY ELEMENTARY

Connally Elementary is located in an impoverished urban section of a large city in the southeastern United States. Over the years Connally had developed a reputation as one of the most troubled primary schools in the district. Even the faculty at the middle school where Connally students would eventually matriculate had a negative perception and low expectations of Connally students. Connally's discouraging image was largely the result of a track record for low performance on state mandated standardized test and a plethora of disciplinary problems at the school. For several years Connally had significant declines in enrollment and the perception was that the academically strong students were leaving. In an effort to make a change at the school the district hired a principal from another state who had a record of improving student performance. My relationship with Connally began four months after Mr. Underdue, the young charismatic and outspoken principal of the school, had taken the helm of the school.

One of the first things I noticed when I walked into the school lobby was a big picture of a train entitled the express to success. While the school was situated within a rather dilapidated section of town with several large vacant buildings, the inside of the school was bright, colorful and inviting. When I asked Mr. Underdue about the express to success he described it as his mantra for parents, students, and teachers. For parents and students the train symbolized the fact that Connally was changing and on the move towards a successful future. For the teachers the train had quite a different meaning. It meant either get on board with "my philosophy and vision for the future of the school or get off and get going". Taken aback by his bluntness I inquired about his philosophy and school plan of action.

EFFECTIVE STRATEGIES WITH SCHOOL FACULTY

Mr. Underdue believed the biggest problem at the school was the atmosphere and school disciplinary problems that involved both students and faculty. The principal made it clear that there were several basic principles and attitudes that teachers must be guided by and embody. Perhaps most importantly Mr. Underdue demanded that teachers always interact with students with a demeanor of respect and care. There had been a pattern of teachers yelling at children, losing their temper and some instances of teachers inappropriately spanking students. Teachers were expected to gain competence in the districts reform model, specifically the curriculum. Teachers were expected to continually highlight student's schoolwork throughout classroom and school bulletin boards. It appeared that Mr. Underdue's plan and vision for the school was clearly articulated and justified given the history of the school. One of the interesting caveats of Mr. Underdue's approach was that at times he seemed to implement his vision for the school with heavy handed interactions with teachers that sometimes bordered on rudeness. When I questioned Mr. Underdue about my perception of his approach he stated that he was convinced that some of the teachers at Connally had no intention of mastering the reform curriculum, highlighting student achievement, or respecting students at the school. Therefore, he stated "I need to make the experience of these teachers as uncomfortable as possible and get them moved out so that all of my students have competent teachers".

At the end of Mr. Underdue's first school year there seemed to be two camps of teachers. One camp liked the changes at Connally while and a small group of teachers who were very displeased with the school's leadership. Everyone I talked to agreed that the discipline issues with the children were greatly improved and test scores were on the rise. At the end of the first year there was significant turnover of teachers at the school. At one of my end of the year meetings with Mr. Underdue he expressed concern about the grades and achievement of the African American male students. We decided that the following year we would focus on a program to increase the involvement and success of African American male students.

INCREASING THE INVOLVEMENT AND SUCCESS OF AFRICAN AMERICAN MALE STUDENTS

Over the past decades, there has been an active debate concerning viability of the public school system in the United States to educate African American male children and provide them with the skills needed to be productive citizens. Disproportionate rates of school failure, drop out, and incarceration all speak to a need to develop interventions, which can account for the structural and ecological factors that impact African American families and African American children (Noguera, 2003). In particular, disproportionately large numbers of African American boys in our city schools are expelled, suspended, relegated to special education programs, and left with fewer personal resources than their European American peers. Although 72% of African American students in America graduate from high school, on the average, in many major cities, over 45% of African American males drop out of high school (Green & Carl, 2000). This rate is higher than any other ethnic/gender group, and African American males drop out of school at a younger age than other groups (Swartz, 2001). In Georgia, the high school completion rate for African American males (defined as the percent of 1997 grade 9 enrollments in graduating class of 2001) was 58%; the overall high school completion rate was 71% (Georgia Public Education Report Card, 2000-01).

In schooling environments, students develop a sense of order, place, and expectations determined in part by the schools' structure and curriculum and by students' interactions with peers, teachers, and parents (Adler, Kless, & Adler, 1992). Educational experiences serve as antecedents to many of the social and economic ills students face later in life. Inequities in school experiences have broad consequences for students' future educational attainment, employment, and family relations. Access to academic experiences through the curriculum, teachers, and other school activities is important for African American males who are already marginalized in school settings (Finn & Cox, 1992; Irvine, 1990). Given the relationship between school failure, high school drop out, delinquency and employment, efforts to address challenges facing African American males needs to focus on a community-based intervention situated school system.

For many African American males, the school system becomes a contentious source of socialization. Most researchers agree that teachers, and peers are especially influential in shaping the school-related behaviors of African American males, too little attention has been given to explaining their under-achievement and antisocial behavior relative to other contextual influences in the school settings. School contexts are often cited as important sources for gendered learning and development. Considerable attention has been given to the affects of gender on schooling experiences and achievement (Adler, Kless, & Adler,

1992). However, Delpit (1988), Fordham and Ogbu (1986) note, school experiences and opportunities are also affected by race and ethnicity, but the intersection between gender and race in these contexts is often overlooked in the educational research literature. Currently, African American males are greatly under-represented in college enrollment, over-represented in incarceration rates and are often under-employed. Educational intervention that focuses on the African American male has the potential to improve some of these devastating statistics.

American schools were designed with two primary functions. The first function of school was to promote and structure the intellectual development of students. The second function of schools was to socialize young people for their roles in society. However, schools are falling short of these goals for our African American male students. One reason for the alienation and poor academic performance of some African American males is that they perceive most school activities as being feminine and irrelevant to their masculine identity. Gender-role socialization that encourages and rewards African American males for not achieving academically is also influencing the crisis (Fordham & Ogbu, 1986). The differences in role expectations are reflected in differential academic performance and effort. Consequently, African American males perceptions of themselves are at odds with their school experience. Researchers contend that there must be an increased presence of committed and successful African American males in school settings to enhance African American boys' academic and social development and to counter inappropriate gender-role socialization (Cunningham, 1993, Holland, 1987).

Many believe that schools are not only failing to meet the particular social and developmental needs of African American males, but are academically abusing them (Lopez, 2003). Young African American males are faced with a number of challenges in their communities and schools yet the strategies that have been proven to be effective are underutilized in addressing the problems (Fashola, 2003; Kunjufu, 2001). Some of these effective strategies include:

- Utilization of male professionals from the community as mentors for students, particularly men of color
- Culturally relevant pedagogy
- Consistent academic support

These are starting points for action that the author used to create a program to meet the needs of African American males at the partner school. Together with funding from the college and the elementary school we created a program called Lionheart to improve disciplinary issues and the achievement of African American males at the elementary school. The goal was to utilize mentoring, academic coaching, and community service to improve the academic achievement and character development of African American males. The project was designed to be culturally relevant and grounded in the utilization of a layered intervention approach. Through a collaborative effort between Georgia State staff (via the Lionheart Program), Georgia State students, high school and elementary school teachers, and parents the Lionheart program sought to reduce the at risk behaviors of urban African American males and increase the academic achievement of its participants.

THE LIONHEART PROGRAM OBJECTIVES

LIONHEART seeks to assist young men of African decent in developing into disciplined, socially responsible, and culturally conscious citizens. The program also wants to empower participants to realize their own personal visions, dreams, and aspirations for their lives. Most importantly, the goal is to assist participants in developing a respect for education, skill development, and academic achievement. Participants engaged in character development and cultural enrichment activities. In addition, the importance of assuming responsibility for the community was emphasized and LIONHEART also provided the opportunity for participants to engage in community improvement activities. It is believed that the achievement of these objectives will contribute to the development of outstanding African-American young men who are academic high achievers, culturally grounded, and committed to making a positive impact on their community.

The principal of the elementary school identified 30 students who had a history of disciplinary problems at the school. The parents of these 30 students children were notified and invited to attend a meeting to learn more about the program. Fifteen parents attended the first meeting where they had the opportunity to learn more about the program. The other students were notified through the mail and were given a consent form granting their child right to participate. 25 3rd and 4th grade students were enrolled into the program. Lionheart consist of both high school and elementary school participants. There is one program coordinator who is compensated to work 20 hours a week with the boys. Once a week the program coordinator of Lionheart met with a group of high school boys attending a local high school. These high school boys served as mentors to the elementary school males. The high school boys received academic coaching, lessons plans, and also plan for the mentoring and after school sessions with the elementary boys. The following day the boys at Connally elementary were bused to the high school where they participated in a two hour after school mentoring program.

The elementary children were extremely excited to participate in the program and were especially excited about being able to go to the high school every week. At the high school they received a lot of positive attention. When they came into the building an announcement was made over the loudspeaker welcoming them. The staff, faculty, administration, and students at the high school welcomed the elementary students with excitement and enthusiasm. During the after school sessions the disciplinary problems were minimal. There were no fights amongst the children, few arguments and the youth did a good job of staying on task.

After two months in the program I met with the principal of the elementary school students to check on the progress for disciplinary referrals among the students. The principal noted that not one of the Lionheart boys had received a disciplinary referral since starting the program. Upon reflecting on it he noted that many of these children were in his office regularly but upon beginning the program he was not aware of any fights or other behavior problems among these boys. The program coordinator and I also talked with the teachers of the elementary students. In general, the teachers noted improvement in the students. In particular, the teachers noted that fighting and disrespectful talk to the adults had completely subsided. The teachers noted that many of the students did still talk out of turn and still had trouble focusing on academic tasks, but overall, they were very pleased with the student behavior.

At the end of the school year the principal reported that there had been no behavior referrals made for any of the Lionheart boys since the program started. In talking with parents, teachers and administrators they held a new level of confidence about them and some of them had found ways to be productive leaders in the school. Attendance had also improved and the teachers reported that the Lionheart students seemed to enjoy school a lot more. However, most of the boys grades remained marginal. This may have been partially due to the fact that program focused largely on character development and discipline.

The goals for the upcoming year will be to increase students' academic achievement and parental involvement in the school. Over the summer the administration created a dedicated parent center and made efforts to focus on parental involvement at Connally. At the end of the second year Connally had made all of the state mandates for achievement, and reached 11 of the 12 district goals. This achievement has Connally designated as a school of distinction in the district. Disciplinary problems continue to be infrequent and the school is in the process of implementing a professional development school model. The principal sited the relationship with the university as a major source of support for transitioning the school from the lowest quartile in the district to the top quartile in achievement in a little over two years.

TRANSITIONING FROM PARTNER SCHOOLS TO PROFESSIONAL DEVELOPMENT SCHOOLS

As the partner school efforts continued to move forward, the deans and chairs discussed taking our partner schools to the next level, specifically

Borthwick, A. C., Stirling, T., Nauman, A. D., & Cook, D. L. (2003). Achieving Successful School-University Collaboration. *Urban Education, 38*(3), 330-371.

Delpit, L. (1988). The silenced dialogue: Power and pedagogy in educating other people's children. *Harvard Educational Review, 58,* 280-298.

Cunningham, M. (1993). Sex role influence on African American males. *Journal of African American Male Studies, 1,* 30-37.

Fashola, O. S. (2003). Developing the talents of african american male students during the nonschool hours. *Urban Education*(4), 398-430.

Finn, J.D., & Cox, D. (1992). Participation and withdrawal among fourth-grade pupils. *American Educational Research Journal, 29,* 141-162.

Fordham, S., & Ogbu, J. (1986). Black students' school success: Coping with the "burden of 'acting white.'" *Urban Review, 18,* 176-206.

Green, R. I., & Carl, B. R., (2000). A reform for troubled times: Takeovers of urban schools. Annals, 569, 56-70.

Holland, S. (1987). Positive primary education for young Black males: Inner-city boys need male role models. *Education Digest, 53,* 6-7.

Lopez, N. (2003). *Hopeful girls, troubled boys: Race and gender disparity in urban education.* New York: Routledge.

Mathie, V. A. (2002). Building academic partnerships in psychology: The Psychology Partnerships Project. American Psychologist, 57(11), 915-926.

Noguera, P. A. (2003). The trouble with black boys: The role and influence of environmental and cultural factors on the academic performance of african american males. *Urban Education*(4), 431-459.

Peel, H. A., & Peel, B. B. (2002). School/University Partnerships: A Viable Model. *International Journal of Educational Management, 16*(7), 319-325.

Ravid, R., & Handler, M. (Eds.). (2001). The many faces of school-university collaboration. Engelewood,CO: Libraries Unlimited.

Sandholtz, J. H. (2002). Inservice training or professional development: Contrasting opportunities in a school/university partnership. Teaching & Teacher Education, 18(7), 815-830.

Swartz, E. (1992). Emancipatory narratives: Rewriting the master script in the school curriculum. *Journal of Negro Education, 61* (3), 341-355.

Teitel, L. (2003). The professional development schools handbook: Starting, sustaining, and assessing partnerships that improve student learning. Thousand Oaks, CA: Corwin Press.

SECTION 2.

EVALUATION OF EDUCATIONAL POLICIES

CHAPTER 4.

Pages 81 - 108
Instructional Language Policies for Creolese Speakers in Guyana: Examining their Social and Academic Outcomes using Comparative Examples from Eight Countries.

Béatrice Boufoy-Bastick
Department of Liberal Arts, French Section,
University of the West Indies,
St. Augustine, Trinidad & Tobago.

CHAPTER 5.

Pages 109 - 142
Policy implications of project evaluation in Guyana:
The case of the Secondary School Reform Project.

Claudette Phoenix
Measurement and Evaluation Unit, National Centre for Educational Resource Development, Ministry of Education, Georgetown, Guyana.

CHAPTER 6.

Pages 143 - 178
Rethinking the Financing
of the Education System in Jamaica.

Disraeli M. Hutton
Department of Educational Studies,
University of the West Indies, Mona, Kingston, Jamaica.

Chapter 4

INSTRUCTIONAL LANGUAGE
POLICIES FOR CREOLESE
SPEAKERS IN GUYANA:
EXAMINING THEIR SOCIAL AND
ACADEMIC OUTCOMES USING
COMPARATIVE EXAMPLES FROM
EIGHT COUNTRIES

BÉATRICE BOUFOY-BASTICK

ABSTRACT

This paper discusses instructional language policies in Creolese-speaking communities in Guyana. It first examines the different roles of English and community languages, the former as the language of instruction in formal education and the latter as interactional languages within Guyana's local communities. It concludes with theoretically based practical notes on language teaching appropriate to each language policy.

The critical issue addressed in this paper is whether the Ministry of Education, through social aspects of its policies, should take responsibility for community languages – and if so, what educational policy options should be considered – or whether the Ministry of Education should ignore community languages in order to focus on early proficiency in the English language.

The controversial decision is to what extent formal education in Guyana should emphasise high English inputs for early academic attainment or prioritise community language inputs for promotion of social equity.

This paper considers three instructional language policies for Creolese-speaking school communities in Guyana and examines their social and academic outcomes. These language policies are: (i) English language immersion, (ii) Transitional language policy and (iii) Bilingual policy. The three policies options are illustrated with comparative examples from Australia, Canada, Fiji, Hawaii, New Zealand, Singapore, Switzerland and the United States of America.

INTRODUCTION

This paper examines instructional language policies in Creolese-speaking school communities in Guyana. It first discusses the different roles of English and community languages, the former as the language of instruction in formal education and the latter as interactional languages within Guyana's local communities. The critical issue addressed in this paper is to what extent formal education in Guyana should emphasise high English inputs for early academic attainment or prioritise community language inputs for the promotion of social equity. The paper considers three instructional language policies, one policy matching each of these extremes and one addressing the middle ground. These instructional language policies are: (i) English language immersion, (ii) Transitional language policy and (iii) Bilingual policy. The three policies options are illustrated with comparative examples from Australia, Canada, Fiji, Hawaii, New Zealand, Singapore, Switzerland and the United States of America.

1. GROWING UP IN GUYANA'S PLURILINGUAL SETTING

Guyana is a rich and vibrant plurilingual setting. This is expressed in the variety of community-specific languages, namely Creolese and Amerindian vernaculars, with each having its own lexical uniqueness and syntactic features. These languages are used in daily personal interactions. They are used to express family closeness and intimacy. They are the languages through which emotions and feelings are expressed. They are the languages in which the child grows, develops and matures before it is time to go to school. Leaving the comfortable emotionally-secure community setting and entering school is a rite of passage: the child moves to a new setting to which he/she has to adapt, to answer to a new authority structure and to respond to different behaviour expectations. This is part of a dual physical and linguistic socialisation process by which the school teaches socially appropriate behavioural and linguistic norms to the child.

From this perspective, the school negates the language and cognitive background of the child and may generate a harsh divide between the community and the school. The homogeneity of the child's monocultural and monolingual community gives way to a dual school/ community compartmentalised sociolingual setting.

COMPARTMENTALISING SOCIOLINGUISTIC SETTING

The sociolinguistic school/community duality exists for all children but manifests itself more acutely among children from non Standard English-speaking communities, namely from Guyana's Creolese or Amerindian communities. This is the duality to which the child needs to accommodate in his/her early years of education. The question for educators is how to reconcile this duality with a psychopedagogically informed language teaching approach that considers the child's affective needs in relation to his/her community language and cognitive needs in relation to the language of formal education. This question is of paramount importance as language development considerably impacts the cognitive growth and educational outcomes of later years. It is this question which is now addressed through three instructional language policies: English immersion, transitional language policy and bilingual policy. To this effect, these three instructional language policies are briefly described with their philosophical and pedagogical concomitants and then evaluated in terms of their social and educational outcomes.

EFFECTS OF INSTRUCTIONAL LANGUAGE POLICIES

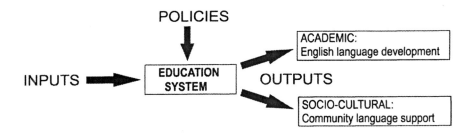

POLICIES

ACADEMIC:
English language development

INPUTS → EDUCATION SYSTEM OUTPUTS

SOCIO-CULTURAL:
Community language support

Source: Original

2. THREE INSTRUCTIONAL LANGUAGE POLICY OPTIONS: AN OVERVIEW

The first option now considered is the English immersion language policy option.

OPTION 1: IMMERSION LANGUAGE POLICY FOR ENGLISH PROFICIENCY IN GUYANA

BASIC PEDAGOGICAL AND PHILOSOPHICAL PREMISES OF ENGLISH LANGUAGE IMMERSION PROGRAMS

English immersion policy assigns English as the sole appropriate means of communication in school, that "the teacher or teachers use English for almost all interactions" (Tabors, 1997). This is the language policy which governs Guyana's education programs (Rickford, 1983, p. 147). This policy negates the educational value of Creolese spoken by many local communities. Conversely, it affirms the role of schooling in eradicating non-standard English-based syntactic forms and supports proficiency in Standard English. The

85

"English only" policy assumes that early English exposure obliterates Creole intrusions and instils grammatically appropriate language behaviours from an early age. The primary school teacher, thus, stands as the language model, the user of school-specific language code which the child is directed to adopt. This directed language modelling assumes a child's intrinsic need to interact with his/her teacher and perhaps may prompt him/her to "impersonate" his/her teacher's speech.

A major postulate in support of early language immersion is that it pre-empts interlingual English-Creolese interference and delineates what language use is appropriate in school. In other words, it postulates that the school takes no responsibility for the teaching of the community language(s).

The success of English language immersion programs depends primarily on support from the community in promoting English and the differential value placed upon English and Creolese; namely highlighting a higher support for English and the lesser value of Creolese. A successful unilingual instructional policy expresses the wish of the community for an academically oriented education which requires mindful conceptualisation and implementation of psychopedagogically informed programmes, such as those from Canada and New Zealand.

SUCCESSFUL LANGUAGE IMMERSION PROGRAMS: EXAMPLES FROM CANADA AND NEW ZEALAND

Language immersion programs have been implemented successfully in culturally and linguistically mixed societies. Canada, for example, initiated innovative French language immersion education programmes for English-speaking elementary school students in the 1960's. Similar language immersion programs, albeit in the indigenous language, were introduced in the Pacific, e.g. in New Zealand (Meade & Podmore, 2002) and Hawaii (Wilson, 1998) in the early 1980s. Both these socioculturally guided language programs were aimed to revive respectively the Maori and Hawaiian vernaculars in indigenous communities, in an attempt to revitalise selected language-embedded cultural traditions among native children. The Maori Education Coordinator (Nancy Gray, personal communication, Sept 2-6, 1996) reported that the fervent Maori community support for the Maori language program, in what is familiarly called 'language nests', led to its extension through to 12th grade. The implementation of this language immersion program is consistent with a philosophical perspective of language, that is language as being the major carrier of culture, and that the culture embedded in the language is highly valued. Notwithstanding that this positioning on community language and culture maintenance may, perhaps, differ from that in Guyana with its seeming de-emphasis of local vernacular maintenance for English-dependent global education, the purpose of language immersion programs is to inculcate preferred high status language habits in children whose language patterns are not yet too deeply imprinted as well as to spur early proficiency in the language of instruction.

School communities are expected to provide language-rich learning environments requiring a multiplicity of language teaching strategies. Examples of these, borrowed from Gattegno's Silent Way (1972; 1976), Asher's (1972; 1977) Total Physical Response and Vygotsky's dialogical communication, are suggested in endnote 1 on *Pedagogical considerations for language immersion programmes.*

OPTION 2: A TRANSITIONAL LANGUAGE POLICY FOR RECONCILING SOCIAL JUSTICE AND ACADEMIC ATTAINMENTS

A transitional language policy requires the language of instruction to be gradually introduced in the early years of schooling. The community language is initially used as the language of class interaction and English is acquired as a foreign or second language. Gradually, English is phased in, and gradually, it becomes the language of instruction. The purpose of this policy is to provide an interim period when children use the community language in culturally relevant interactions, and learn the language of instruction as an additional language. Transitional language policies recognise the cultural value of the community language and also stress the role of formal education in bringing children into the English-speaking global community.

Transitional language policies have been implemented differently in linguistically diverse states to accommodate the various compositions of their base culture. Fiji and Australia in Oceania provide two illustrative contrasting examples of differently conceptualised and operationalised transitional language policies, namely, a culturally child-sensitive language policy in Fiji and a social justice-directed policy in Australia.

A CULTURALLY CHILD-SENSITIVE APPROACH TO ENGLISH ACQUISITION: THE FIJI EXAMPLE

Bauan Fijian is an official language in Fiji. It is the mother tongue of native Fijians and expresses the "vaka viti" (Fijian way) clan-based lifestyle and cultural values; it is the expression of the Fijian cultural identity. English, by contrast, is the colonial language which has evolved as a lingua franca between two linguistically and culturally diverse communities, the native Fijians and the Indo-Fijians, the latter being descendants of Indian indentured labourers (Lotherington-Woloszyn, 1991a, p. 399; Mugler, 1996, p. 275). English is the expression of Fiji's shared civic identity and is the common ethnically-independent language of instruction. Rural communities, however, speak either a Fijian vernacular or Fiji Hindi, called Fiji Baat (a Bojphuri dialect). So the first three years of primary schooling are associated with the acquisition of a new linguistic code. On entering Grade 4 children are expected to possess the basic language tools for English-only scholastic instruction. Unsurprisingly, this aim is differentially met at the end of Grade 3. Higher English proficiency is achieved in diglossic urban communities which can draw on higher out-of-school English inputs, compared to those monolingual island communities that have negligible English out-of-school inputs (Boufoy-Bastick, 2000; 2003; Lotherington-Woloszyn, 1991b, p. 148). Functionality in English remains limited among rural/island children for whom English is a foreign language, not a second language, and this is evidenced in their lower language attainments in national examinations in later years (Boufoy-Bastick, 2003). In contrast, however, it demonstrates the vitality of the culture-embedded community languages.

AN ENGLISH LANGUAGE POLICY FOR SOCIAL JUSTICE: THE AUSTRALIAN EXAMPLE

The transitional language policy in Australia differs markedly from that of Fiji in its culturally inclusive approach. It rests fundamentally upon core Australian cultural values expressing social equity. This transitional language policy acknowledges the linguistic background of the child and the different language needs of native children and children from a Non-English Speaking Background (NESB). The Australian transitional language policy is geared to non-native speakers and aims to remedy their English language 'deficit'. The NESB children's lack of English is perceived as a deficit since English is the language of instruction as from Grade 1 and academic attainments are contingent upon mastery of English. These NESB children receive English as a

Second Language (ESL) instruction in "sheltered" classes in which programs offered specifically to "Students with Limited English Proficiency" (SLEP) are designed "to provide in-class or pullout instruction for any school-age children whose language competence is insufficient to participate fully in normal school instruction" (Richards & Rogers, 2001, pp. 206-207). The purpose of these programmes is not so much to learn English as an end in itself, but to provide the learning tools to understand and communicate information (Richards & Rogers, 2001). From this perspective, the Australian SLEP programs can be said to be pedagogically grounded in Content-Based Instruction (CBI) and socially geared to provide a "level playing field", that is to enable each child to have, what the Australians familiarly call, "a fair go" in an egalitarian multicultural society (Boufoy-Bastick, 1997; 2003, p. 124).

These two brief descriptions contrast the different socio-educational orientations of two humanistically influenced English language policies. They both evidence a governmental concern for social fairness, albeit within a staunch monolingual framework. It is, however, this same social principle that has elsewhere mandated the implementation of bilingual policies.

OPTION 3: BILINGUAL POLICIES FOR REVALUING LOCAL CULTURES WITHIN NATIONAL AND SUPRA-NATIONAL PARAMETERS

Most modern societies are multicultural. A functional, socially integrated, multicultural society recognises the cultural specificities and the differential learning needs of each constituent social or ethnic group. At first sight, these two principles of social integration and social specificity may be seemingly mutually exclusive but they are the ideological tenets of cultural diversity upon which bilingual educational initiatives are founded (Miramontes, Nadeau & Commins, 1997, p. 23).

Bilingual language programs are social education programs aimed at partitioning language space into English and the community language. Their aims are twofold. On one hand, bilingual language programs aim to promote English for the purpose of maintaining a harmonious multicultural society through ease of inter-ethnic communication, and on the other, to maintain the community language(s) for intra-ethnic communication and cultural maintenance. These two fundamental aims informed the design of prominent bilingual programs, such as the Magnet School initiative in the United States and a core Asian value-anchored curriculum in Singapore.

**SUPPORTING BILITERACY
AWARENESS IN THE UNITED
STATES: THE MAGNET SCHOOLS
EXAMPLE**

US magnet schools (not to be confused with the 1997 "magnet schools" primary school project in Guyana) were open as bilingual schools for both monolingual English-speaking and non-English speaking children from pre-Kindergarten through primary schooling. Understandably, they were initially established in school districts with predominantly bilingual populations, such as in California and the North-East. These were two-way immersion programs which focused on developing biliteracy in English and Spanish and which promoted an appreciation of both Anglo-American and Hispanic cultures (Endnote 2). In the districts in which they were established, these bilingual programs receive warm support from both the language minority group and the English-speaking professional class. It should be noted that the first language remains the medium by which literacy skills are first introduced, although pedagogic materials are available in both languages. The resultant material duplication has, however, cost implications. Because these are "one teacher-one language" bilingual programs, costs are further increased by the need for a greater number of teachers. As a result of the higher program costs, priority is often given to non English-speaking children or else multi-grade classes are opened. Such measures have enabled some "magnet schools", such as the English-Creole school for Haitian immigrant children in Cambridge, Massachusetts, to sustain their bilingual programs into the higher primary school grades.

In contrast to the selective costly US bilingual programs, Singapore runs cost-effective bilingual education programs which enhance the population's current bilingualism.

PROMOTING CORE ASIAN VALUES - ANCHORED BILINGUALISM IN SINGAPORE

Singapore's compulsory schooling for children aged 6 to 12 was only introduced last year in 2003. Pre-schools for children between the ages of 3 and 6 are run by the private sector, for example community foundations, religious, social and commercial organizations. Schools teach two languages English and one of the three ethnic languages, Malay for ethnic Malays, Mandarin for ethnic Chinese and Tamil for ethnic East Indians. English remains the main language of instruction and the lingua franca between the three main ethnic groups. The ethnic languages are given mother tongue status, irrespective of the child's home dialect, such as Chinese may be Hakka or Hokien speakers but are taught Mandarin in school while Indians may be Urdu or Telagu speakers and are required to study Tamil. This policy serves three purposes: cutting teaching cost by providing one language teacher for each ethnic group in a school, fostering ethnic group unity in an ethnically diverse society and protecting selected core Asian values from the Western culture embedded in the English language (Boufoy-Bastick, 1997). So the teaching of the ethnic language mostly serves a social purpose while the teaching of English serves an economic purpose, namely to ensure participation in the global economy. However, instructional programs use predominantly English as the main language of interaction between teachers and children and the mother tongue is given specific instructional time.

As an illustrative example of a Singaporean instructional language program, a brief description of the bilingual English-Mandarin program of the early childhood centre run by Singapore Polytechnic. All teachers at the centre were bilingual and used both English and Mandarin while interacting with children. To a varying degree, there was a certain amount of interlanguage in informal teacher-child interaction. Nonetheless, teachers were to be addressed respectfully by their formal Chinese titles, for example Lao-Tse. Formal instructional activities were carried out either in English or in Mandarin. For instance, basic literacy and numeracy skills were taught in English during the English class while Chinese character recognition, the use of the abacus were taught in Mandarin – literally 'taught', as the Chinese support direct transmission teaching.

Beside skill teaching, the program focused on cultural transmission and biculturality, so children's songs were taught in Standard English (not in Singlish as spoken in the community) and in Mandarin Chinese (avoiding dialectal intrusions). Instructions were given either in English or in Mandarin. Asian/Western biculturality was reinforced through compartmentalising preferred English and Asian cultural practices, such as using trainer chopsticks for a governmentally approved healthy and balanced Chinese diet and learning English nursery rhymes for exposure to Western culture. In sum, the instructional language programs at Singapore Polytechnic were designed to prepare young children to internalise two cultural codes (East and West) and move with fluidity between them as determined by the social context.

Now, let's consider the implications of these instructional language policies for the Ministry of Education in Guyana. The crux of the matter is whether the Ministry of Education through the social aspects of its policies should take responsibility for community languages, namely Creolese and Amerindian vernaculars, and if so what educational policy should be considered, namely a transitional or a bilingual policy, or whether the responsibility of the Ministry of Education should only be for the official language of instruction. What need to be considered when choosing an instructional language policy are the social and educational implications. Socially, the maintenance of both languages through a bilingual policy, be it transitional or maintained into higher school grades, acknowledges the specific linguistic code of the child's social network and its inter-relational and affective role as well as establishing English as the language of formal education. By contrast, an English-only language policy focuses on the academic returns from high English inputs and de-emphasises the interactional aspect of language. The choice is either to prioritise the social or the academic aspect of formal education.

CONCLUSION

This paper has highlighted some critical issues with regard to instructional language policies by providing an overview of language policies implemented in different parts of the world.

The first instructional language policy option which was presented was the English-only language policy. This option suggests total language immersion in English and ignores the Creolese community language(s) and has the intention of speeding English acquisition and of promoting higher attainments in English upon which later academic attainments are built (endnote 3). Given this momentous academic advantage of the English-only policy, parents from the "educated" Guyanese elite in Georgetown support this policy. However, selecting the English language policy option with its corollary of suppressing Creolese implies suppressing the community culture and Creolese is the "life blood" of Guyana's culture. The danger is that a strict "English only" language policy obliterates the community language so might destabilise the social fabric of the community and jeopardise social harmony. It expresses a devaluing of the community language and, to some extent a devaluing of the local culture. This raises the fundamental question which is not so much whether the Ministry of Education wants to maintain the language, but whether they want to maintain the culture.

The second instructional language policy option is a transitional bilingual policy in early childhood education. The objectives of this policy are both psychological and educational. Psychologically, this policy recognises the child's out-of-school inter-relational network. This network has been developed through the Creolese language which has, thus far, met the child's basic communicational needs. Although a transitional language policy can be operationalised in various ways to fit in with the local Guyanese context, it suggests maintaining Creolese for informal interaction and acquiring basic literacy and numeracy skills in English. This assumes language compartmentalisation, with the recognition of Creolese in informal teacher-child interaction and the adoption of English for formal basic instruction. The 2000 National Centre for Educational Resource Development (NCERD) Grade 1 syllabus acknowledges this contextual language duality and suggests language-awareness activities, for example by comparing both phonological and grammatical aspects of Creolese and Standard English. This implicitly recognises English as a second language which is to become the accepted language of instruction on entering primary school. Pedagogically, this supports Lisa Delpit's student-sensitive teaching approach in that "Teachers need to support the language that students bring to school, provide them input from an additional code, and give them the opportunity to use the new code in a non-threatening, real communicative context" (1995, p. 53). In short, the transitional language policy uses a child-centred approach which fulfils a social and an academic objective, the former by valuing the community culture, the latter by providing the English input for higher academic attainments.

The third instructional language policy option is a bilingual policy. This policy bears resemblance to that used implicitly in homes where each parent is from a different language group. Their children are raised using both languages and are likely to become balanced bilingual speakers. This childrearing behaviour is based on the principle of "one person, one language", that is the child learns to identify each parent with a distinct language code. Similarly, bilingual programs are based on a "one language, one context" principle. This principle guides Guyana's educational programs which associate acrolectal English with the language of formal contexts and basilectal Creolese with the language of informal interact ional communications (Holbrook & Holbrook, 2002; Hosein & Mohamed, 1994; Rickford, 1983). The issue is how best children can maximise social and academic returns by acquiring two context-dependent linguistic codes needed to function adeptly in Guyana's diglossic society.

ENDNOTES

ENDNOTE 1: *PEDAGOGICAL CONSIDERATIONS FOR LANGUAGE IMMERSION PROGRAMMES*

Teaching language to young children requires a specific activity-directed interactional approach. This may suggest the suitability of selected pedagogical strategies borrowed from innovative second language teaching; instructional methods such as, Gattegno's Silent Way (1972; 1976), Asher's (1972; 1977) Total Physical Response. It also suggests promoting dialogic communication for language construction using a lexical approach to early childhood language education (Lewis, 1977; Willis, 1990). These three approaches prioritise language learning over language teaching: the Silent Way with listening, TPR by doing and dialogical communication by two-way verbal interaction.

The Silent Way is a second language teaching approach emphasising the primacy of learning over teaching; it is premised upon the child's commitment to discovery and to create. The Silent Way uses a lexical syllabus and prioritises the development of a "functional vocabulary". Vocabulary-building is hence crucial to the child's activity-based language development. In this teaching approach, the teacher acts indirectly to spur the child's interest, for example by providing coloured rods for the child to experiment and by displaying charts and visual aids to elicit the child's physical and verbal responses. The verbal responses are then used as interactional signals to prompt the teacher to provide correct language cues. This method shows "a strong focus on accurate repetition of sentences modeled initially by the teacher and a movement through guided elicitation exercises to freer communication" (Richards and Rogers, 2001, p. 89).

Similar strategies from Total Physical Response (TPR) can be successfully applied to English immersion language programmes. TPR is an activity-based language teaching method which claims language is learnt through actions (Asher, 1977) and commands (Asher, 1972). As in the Silent Way, TPR prioritises kinesthetic engagement, but in TPR the child responds first to language physically by carrying out an instruction. TPR hence prioritises listening over speaking and it is the sustained oral language exposure which promotes the child's language appropriation. This method is particularly suited to early childhood language programmes as it focuses on vocabulary acquisition through action-based drills. Although drills have negative behaviorist connotations like conditioning, these establish a lexical basis upon which more syntactically sophisticated language structures can be introduced. It is with this purpose in mind that Elaine Ray extended TPR into TPR Story-telling in the late 1980's (Marsh, 1997). She used enthralling stories as media for listening, acting out and re-telling by contextualising the acquired language, that is for intensifying the child's further language learning by providing narrative and descriptive modes.

Promoting dialogic communication for language development is grounded in Vygotsky's (1962) sociocultural theory of language. Language is held as the symbolic tool used by the teacher to direct the child through an exploratory learning activity, that is to surreptitiously lead him/her through the various problem-solving steps through collaborative verbal exchanges. This pedagogical strategy known as "*scaffolding*" involves "a dialogically constituted interpsychological mechanism that promotes the novices' internalisation of knowledge co-constructed in shared activity" (Donato, 1994, p. 41). The young child's cognitive development is thus mediated by language through social and interactional processes. The child's increasing learning autonomy is later evidenced by the child's reliance on "private speech", known in Jamaica as "dialoguing with oneself". This is when the child verbalises his/her thoughts while engaged in an activity. As Mitchell and Myles (1998, p. 161) remarked "this extended spoken accommodation to action provides evidence about the role of language in problem-solving and self-regulation" and the gradual "*appropriation*" of language in "intra-mental" learning (p. 162).

Vygotskian thinking permeates most humanistic language learning approaches such as the Whole Language approach prominent in the 1990's. First, it conceptualises language from a socio-interactional perspective (Lowe, 2000), as the medium for internal interaction for private and inner speech. Secondly, it conceptualises language from a constructivist perspective, as socially constructed for creating meaning through interaction. The Whole Language approach stresses authentic communication and the importance of meaning making; it holds language as a social activity (Richards & Rogers, 2001; Rigg, 1991, p. 523). The Whole Language approach is directed by the child's needs and interests. These principles guided the development of an early English immersion literacy program in Fiji (Grades 1 to 3) called the "Book Flood" in the early 1980's. This was a New Zealand initiative for English literacy immersion implemented by the Institute of Education at the University of the Pacific. One hundred high-interest low vocabulary books were donated to selected classes in eight rural schools. Teachers were trained in how best to create an enriching and engrossing collaborative language experience for the children by having them sitting on the floor in a semi-circle listening during the teacher's reading. Each reading sequence was followed by a discussion on the plot, the character and explanation of new vocabulary. Evaluation of the "Book Flood" experiment showed an "unusually rapid" rate of English language growth (Elley, Cutting, Mangubhai & Hugo, 1996; Elley, 2000). To facilitate the sustainability of the program teachers were trained to make their own reading books, called "Big Books" using stories created by the children. A similar Book Flood initiative in 1985, called "Reading and English Acquisition Program" (REAP) was highly successful in Singapore in making children confident users of English (Elley, Cutting, Mangubhai & Hugo, 1996).

ENDNOTE 2: *US BILINGUAL MAGNET SCHOOLS EXAMPLE*

The US early childhood "magnet school" program, (Pre-K), aims to develop primarily listening and speaking skills in two languages, usually English and Spanish, with the intent to promote communicative language acquisition. These programs use a team of bilingual primary teachers trained in discovery-learning methods, such as the popular Montessori Method. The implementation of the bilingual programs range from 'one-teacher, one-language' to simultaneous translation of objects or commands. So, children learn to recognise and respond appropriately to verbal cues. Pedagogic materials includes the use of bilingual books for exposure to the written system, songs, nursery rhymes and labels (for example, Jack and the Beanstalk or Juan y los frijoles magicos; Little Red Riding Hood or Caperucita Roja). Vocabulary is explored by learning simultaneously the names of colours and objects in the two languages.

ENDNOTE 3: *RATIONALE FOR "ENGLISH-ONLY" INSTRUCTIONAL LANGUAGE POLICY*

Young children develop language through exposure; within limits, the bigger the input the faster the language acquisition. Teachers in nursery education are the major language input providers and the main person with whom children interact. Through this interaction, children acquire language and develop their verbal expression (Krashen, 1992). Krashen and Terrell (1983) assert that interaction is a "natural" way by which children unconsciously develop their language abilities, that is they appropriate a primary human interpersonal communication tool. The children's motivation to communicate with their teacher, together with their capacity for language acquisition, provides a rationale for early English-only language policy. This policy can be implemented with greater ease at pre-school as the children's verbal fluency in the home vernacular is still limited and the teacher thus becomes a major source of language input and a model.

REFERENCES

Asher, J. (1972). Children's first language as a model of second language learning. *Modern Language Journal, 56*, 133-139.

Asher, J. (1977). *Learning Another Language through Actions: The Complete Teacher's Guide Book* (2nd ed., 1982). Los Gatos, CA: Sky Oaks Productions.

Boufoy-Bastick, B. (1997). Using language policies to highlight and contrast the values that shape multicultural societies: Examples from Singapore and Australia. *Australian Journal of Education, 41*(1), 59-76.

Boufoy-Bastick, B. (2000). *Storying cultural specificities of ESL teaching in Fiji: A grounded narrative.* Paper presented at the 29th Annual meeting of the Society for Cross-Cultural Research, New Orleans, February 22-27th, 2000.

Boufoy-Bastick, B. (2003). *Academic Attainments and Cultural Values.* Munich: Lincom Europa Academic Publishers.

Boufoy-Bastick, B. (2003). *Socio-historical Precursors of Economic Rationalism in Australian Education.* Kingston, Jamaica: Stoneman & Lang.

Delpit, L. (1995). *Other People's Children. Cultural Conflict in the Classroom.* New York: The New Press.

Donato, R. (1994). Collective scaffolding in second language learning. In J.P. Lantoff & G. Appel (Eds.) *Vygotskian approaches in second language research* (pp. 35-56). Norwood, NJ: Ablex Publishing Corporation.

Elley, W. B. (2000). The potential of book floods for raising literary levels. *International Review of Education, 46*(3-4), 233-255.

Elley, W., Cutting, B. Mangubhai, F. & C. Hugo (1996). *Lifting Literacy Levels with Story Books: Evidence from the South Pacific, Singapore, Sri Lanka, and South Africa.* Paper presented at the World Conference on Literacy (Philadelphia, PA, March 12-15, 1996).

Gattegno, C. (1972). *Teaching Foreing Languages in Schools: The Silent Way* (2nd ed.). New York: Education Solutions.

Gattegno, C. (1976). *The Common Sense of Teaching Foreign Languages.* New York: Education Solutions.

Gay, G. (2000). *Culturally Responsive Teaching. Theory, Research and Practice.* New York: Teachers College Press.

Gray, N. (1996, Sept 2-6): *UN international conference on the 'Rights of Indigenous Peoples',* Forum Secretariat, Suva, Fiji (personal communication).

Krashen, S. & Terrell, T. (1983). *The Natural Approach: Acquisition in the Classroom.* Oxford: Pergamon.

Krashen, S. (1992). *Fundamentals of Language Education.* Beverley Hills, CA: Laredo.

La Forge, P.G. (1983). *Counseling and Culture in Second Language Acquisition.* Oxford: Pergamon.

Lewis, M. (1997). *Implementing the Lexical Approach.* London: Language Teaching Publications.

Lotherington-Woloszyn, H. (1991). A critical review of the ESL curriculum in Fiji. In C. Benson (Ed.) Proceedings of the *Fourth South Pacific Seminar in Education: Pacific Curriculum* (pp. 144-150). Suva, Institute of Education, University of the South Pacific.

Lotherington-Woloszyn, H. (1991). Literacy in ESL: Pedagogical and Cultural Pathfindings in Fiji. *BAND91*(1), 396-412.

Lowe, K. (2000). Lifting the lid on early childhood literacy. *AECA Research in Practice Series, 7*(1).

Meade, A. & Podmore, V. (2002). *Report on Early Childhood Education Policy Co-ordination under the Auspices of the Department/ Ministry of Education*: A Case Study of New Zealand. Early Childhood and Family Policy Series. Paris: UNESCO.

Miramontes, O., Nadeau A. & Commins, N. (1997). *Restructuring School for Linguistic Diversity*. New York: Teachers College Press.

Mugler, F. (1996). 'Vernacular' language teaching in Fiji. In F. Mugler and J. Lynch (Eds.) *Pacific Languages in Education* (pp. 227-287). Suva: Institute of Pacific Studies.

NCERD (2000). *Language Arts. Curriculum Guide Level 1*. Georgetown: Materials Production Unit.

Rigg, P. (1991). Whole language in TESOL. *TESOL Quaterly, 25*(3), 521-542.

Rogoff, B. (2003). *The Cultural Nature of Human Development*. Oxford: Oxford University Press.

Tabors, P. (1997). *One Child, Two Languages. A Guide for Preschool Educators*. Baltimore: Paul H. Brookes Publishing Co.

Vygotsky, L.S. (1962). *Thought and Language*. Cambridge, MA: MIT Press.

Willis, J.D. (1990). *The Lexical Syllabus*. London: Collins COBUILD.

Wilson, W. (1998). The sociopolitical context of establishing Hawaiian-medium education. *Language, Culture and Curriculum, 11*(3), p. 325-38.

BÉATRICE BOUFOY-BASTICK

Chapter 5

POLICY IMPLICATIONS OF PROJECT EVALUATION IN GUYANA: THE CASE OF THE SECONDARY SCHOOL REFORM PROJECT

CLAUDETTE PHOENIX

ABSTRACT

Over the years, Guyana like many other countries, has been initiating various reform programmes to improve the quality of secondary education. Guyana's most recent secondary reform programme – the Secondary School Reform Project (1996-2004) is the focus of this chapter.

This multiphase project which, according to its main objective, sought to improve the quality, relevance and equity of secondary education in Guyana, was piloted in twelve schools in six administrative regions. The majority of the schools were lower secondary schools. In order to appreciate the introduction of the reform, a brief report on the history and the overview of Guyana's education system is given. In this history, various aspects of secondary education are discussed. Among them are the three main types of secondary schools, and the programme offered at each, the ramifications of allocating students to the types of secondary schools, and a brief history of other secondary reform programmes undertaken in Guyana prior to the Secondary School Reform Project (SSRP).

Self - evaluations done during and at the end of the project revealed that the project enjoyed both successes and failures. However, after four years into the project, there was public concern that the project was not meeting academic expectations. An independent evaluation, using a perception questionnaire, an attainment test of English Language and the results of the National Third Form Examination for three years - 2001 to 2003, for English Language and Mathematics, was done. While the perception questionnaire and the attainment test were administered to a sample of both SSRP and non-SSRP students in a section of an administrative region, the results of the National Third Form Examination were administered to both sets of students in the regions where SSRP schools were found.

An analysis of the results of the perception questionnaire revealed that students of SSRP schools had lower perception of their teaching than students in matched non-SSRP schools, while that of the attainment test found that the same group of SSRP students had lower attainments in English Language than their peers in non-SSRP schools. The results of the National Third Form Examinations revealed that the project was unable to raise the academic attainment of its students relative to those of non-SSRP schools. The means of the examination results of SSRP students were lower for both Mathematics and English Language. Based on the results of the independent evaluation it was surmised that the project did not realize its expectations.

Certain education policy decisions resulted from the pilot of Secondary Schools Reform Project. Five of these were discussed in this chapter. These decisions have all been implemented in the secondary schools across Guyana.

SECONDARY EDUCATION IN GUYANA

Education has always been viewed by most governments as one of the most important factors which leads to the development of a country. The government of Guyana is one that holds this view. This is evident in Guyana's Education Policy Document (1995, p.6) which states that Education is a critical factor in the national effort to promote productivity and economic growth and to enhance the quality of life of the Guyanese people. In pursuit of this policy, free education is offered in Guyana from the early childhood education cycle to the end of the secondary cycle.

Both the early childhood education and the primary education cycles lay important foundations for success at the secondary level. Secondary school teachers are expected to build on these foundations and prepare students to take up the mantle of good citizens at the end of their secondary schooling. It is the general belief that teachers operating at the secondary level must be skilled, qualified and patient inter alia since they are given the delicate task of preparing their students with skills which will equip them for the world of work or for future learning. Embedded in these skills are various attributes which graduates of secondary schools must display in the next stage of life. Some of these are to:

- display problem solving skills
- adjust to rapidly changing technology
- display functionally literate and numerate skills

It may be posited that if graduates of secondary schools demonstrate the attributes listed above, then they would be better able to participate meaningfully in the world of work and thus contribute to the development of the nation.

For over a century, secondary schools have met work-force needs of Guyana and have given a steady supply of students to institutions of further learning. In this way, the secondary schools have served as 'stepping stones' for the world of work and further education. They were seen as playing a pivotal role in the development of a society.

112

Despite this assertion, it is now the general view that secondary schools are not providing students with the essential knowledge and skills they need for the work force nor to adequately access post secondary education. It is posited that many secondary schools are no longer considered to be effectively achieving their main objective of adequately preparing students for the work force and for post secondary education. The general complaint is that most of these institutions are failing and so educators are turning to educational reform strategies to solve the problem of failing schools.

The fundamental goal of education reform is to improve student achievement. It also aims at providing quality education for all children. Quality education is intended to enable persons to become effective thinkers thus enabling them to function as productive members of society. Quality education is considered necessary for an educated work force and critical to societal development.

For most Guyanese students, the secondary school offers the final stage of their formal general education. Only a minority of these students continue their post secondary schooling in vocational schools, colleges, specialized schools, universities and professional schools. The range of continuing educational opportunities are much wider in developed countries than in developing countries like Guyana since they have very few post secondary institutions from which to choose. Still, both developed and developing countries have used and are still using active reform strategies as a basis of improving the quality of educational delivery at all levels.

Reform efforts have evolved over the years. Educational reform strategies have been applied internationally to improve various areas of secondary education. For example, in Ghana, reform efforts were undertaken to introduce a more vocationally - orientated curriculum into the Junior Secondary Schools (Osei, 2003). In the Republic of Kazakstan, reform strategies were used to improve various aspects of secondary education with the hope of improving the economic and social well-being of the newly created country (DeYoung & Balzhan, 1996; DeYoung & Valyayeva, 1997).

Reform strategies that involved on-line delivery with motivation for participation were also undertaken to improve the teaching practices of teachers at the secondary level. The Inquiry Learning Forum described by Moore and Barab (2002), as an "Internet – based professional development environment designed to support teachers in sharing and evolving their teaching practices" was intended to improve secondary education using Information Technology.

The Secondary School Reform Project was introduced in 1996 mainly to improve the quality of education offered to lower secondary school students in Guyana. This was necessary since there was a great disparity in the delivery of education at the various types of secondary schools which resulted in parents and students alike decrying these lower secondary schools. A brief look at the types of secondary schools will enlighten the reader of the secondary education system in Guyana.

THE SUB-SYSTEMS OF SECONDARY EDUCATION IN GUYANA

Secondary education is offered at three main types of secondary schools – the General Secondary, discrete Community High and the Secondary Department of Primary Schools. The General secondary type is divided into Senior and Junior Secondary Schools with the Multilateral Schools falling into both categories.

Senior secondary schools are considered to be the highest. Here, a seven year programme, leading to the Caribbean Advanced Proficiency Examination (CAPE) or the General Certificate of Education (GCE) Advanced Level, is offered. Students are exposed to a range of academic subjects that are complimented by pre-vocational subjects. After the first five years of schooling students who obtained at least five subjects with high grades at, the most, two sittings at the Caribbean Secondary Education Certificate (CSEC) General Proficiency Level or / and the General Certificate of Education (GCE) Examination are given the opportunity to pursue advanced studies.

A five year programme is offered at the Junior Secondary Schools. This programme also gives students the opportunity to study a range of academic subjects and some pre-vocational subjects leading to the CSEC General Proficiency Examination. Those who are suitably qualified can gain entry to senior secondary schools and pursue the advanced studies offered there.

A four-year programme, biased towards the acquisition of pre-vocational skills, is offered at the Community High School. During the first three years both pre-vocational and academic subjects are taught. Prior to 2001 students were given the opportunity to write the Secondary Schools Proficiency Examination – Part I. The subjects offered were Mathematics, English Language, and Social Studies. Science was optional. Children who were successful were given the opportunity to attend a Junior Secondary School. The others continued to the fourth year of the programme, specializing in pre-vocational areas of their choice. At the end of that year they were given the opportunity to write the Secondary Schools Proficiency Examination – Part II. This generally marked the completion of this type of programme. Some students went on to technical-vocational institutions while others entered the world of work. In some Community High Schools a five year academic programme is offered, in a limited number of subjects, to students with the intellectual capability.

In 2005 a new assessment 'The Basic Competency Certificate Programme' was piloted with Grade Ten (Form Four) students. This assessment will replace the Secondary Schools Proficiency Examination Parts I and II.

The Secondary Department of Primary Schools (Primary Tops) have a similar programme to that offered in the discrete Community High School.

Students are allocated to these types of secondary schools based on their performance at the Secondary Schools Entrance Examination (SSEE) This examination which was renamed, in September 2006 as the National Grade Six Assessment, uses a norm referenced mode to compare candidates' performances on a battery of papers. Students' performance, as per subject tested, is standardized using the Stanford – Binet IQ formula. Total scores are presented on a ranked list. Students are then allocated to the secondary schools which are also ranked. The Senior Secondary Schools are the highest ranked schools while the Secondary Departments of Primary Schools are the lowest.

The 'cut off' points for allocation to secondary schools vary from one administrative region to the next. For instance, a student with a given final score may be awarded a place at a Community High School in Georgetown (Region Four) while another student with the same final score may be awarded a place at a Junior Secondary School in another administrative region, for example, Linden (Region Ten). This is so because the award system depends on the availability of places in the schools of the administrative regions. One can safely conclude then, that some students with similar final scores at the same sitting of the Secondary Schools Entrance Examination may be allocated to different levels of secondary schools.

The crucial point is that even though children may gain the same final score at the same sitting, of the Secondary Schools Entrance Examination, (SSEE) they may not be exposed to the same type of secondary programme. Hence some students with the same results at the same sitting of the examination are given different educational opportunities.

Those who are awarded places at Community High Schools or at Primary Tops are at a disadvantage. The students allocated to these schools, which are referred to as lower secondary schools, are not normally given the opportunity to write the Caribbean Secondary Education Certificate (CSEC) Examinations or the General Certificate of Education (GCE) Examinations.

Students who are awarded places at lower secondary schools are stigmatised in terms of their academic potential. They are perceived by the general public as students with a plethora of difficulties. Jennings et al (1995, p.x) found that most of the 89% of youths who are functionally illiterate in Guyana were from Community High Schools and Secondary Departments of Primary Schools.

Many opined that the problem exists because the students are often not motivated to do the work offered at school.

According to Farrant(1990; p.115), motivation is all-important for getting children to want to learn. Once children want to learn, the battle is half-won. However it is difficult to make these students learn. They seem to have poor self concept and see themselves as failures. Further, since some parents feel that they are better off contributing the family's labour force, they are encouraged to become school 'drop-outs' too and engage in some economic activity to boost family earnings.

The general belief is that the Community High School programme has not lived up to expectations.

THE COMMUNITY HIGH SCHOOL PROGRAMME

This programme which came on stream in 1973 was a major education reform programme in Guyana. It focused on the development of technical/vocational skills that could enhance the development of the country. It was intended that students in the catchment area where these schools were located would benefit from the programme.

The Community High School programme was designed to meet the needs of the community. Ministry of Education (1977, p.9) in referring to Community High Schools notes that:

It is a school that will enable those who complete the programme to find paid employment, to become self employed or to continue studies mainly of a technical/vocational nature in another institution such as the (Government) Technical Institute or (Guyana) School of Agriculture.

The broad aim has caused Bovell (1976, p.1) to single out the following two specific aims as important:

(a) Orienting the school population to occupational skills necessary for the economic and social development of Guyana.

(b) Providing organising skills which prepare young people for self employment in accordance with their skills and interests and the observed needs of particular communities.

These aims played a great role in the development of new curricula which took into consideration the needs of the community. Coupled with this new curricula, came new learning experiences. These along with the work-study experiences were expected to play an important role in the development of the child, the community, and the country as a whole.

The goals of feeding, clothing and housing the nation were seen as avenues for developing the young nation Guyana. Attention was paid to the acceleration of training in skills, which were necessary for the social and economic development of the country. Paul (1979),

120

noted that this acceleration would have been done by continuing the kind of education which would provided manpower for professional and sub-professional skills, and by concentrating on training which would equip young people to take advantage of the large number of job situations which would be made available in technical and semi-technical fields.

In order to accommodate this programme, seven Community High Schools were to be built with funds from the World Bank. Under this project, ten five-year secondary schools were to be converted to multilateral – type schools. That is, schools which gave students the opportunity to study a wider range of subjects other than traditional Arts and Science subjects. Some of these new subjects, which were in the technical vocational areas were Agricultural Science, Industrial arts and Home Economics.

When the Community High School programme was introduced, many stakeholders were enthusiastic. After conducting a research on a sample of students from the first batch of graduates from Community High Schools, Paul (1979) concluded that the programme was a success, but it was not sustainable. The inability of the programme to satisfy expectations probably influenced the Minister of Education, Dr. Bisnauth's statement (1999, p.1) that the Community High School has not lived up to the expectations of those who instituted it in the 1970's; neither has it lived up to the expectations of parents of students. The Minister also posited that statistics reveal that Community High schools and Secondary Department of Primary Schools often have a higher dropout rate than that of General Secondary Schools even though the latter has a higher enrolment figure.

The Community High School programme indeed, has not lived up to expectations. This is due mainly to years of neglect of proper maintenance or replacement of materials for training. Many of the training facilities at these schools are generally unusable or antiquated. As a result students do not acquire the much needed practical skills, which is necessary for prevocational training. Even though the programme at these schools, which is more pre-vocational and less academic, are geared to prepare students to enter the labour market upon graduation, many of them find themselves at a disadvantage when competing for jobs in the skilled labour fields with students from general secondary schools. This is due mainly to the perception of employers, who feel that students who graduate from the Community High School programme are less capable and talented than students from the other types of secondary schools.

The programme is a disappointment to them since many parents felt that their children, on graduating from this programme, would have been able to obtain jobs easily. The first set of students who graduated found it much easier to access jobs than students who graduated in the latter periods. Many students from the Community High School programme leave schools functionally illiterate. A study conducted by Jennings et al (1995:x) found that 89% of 'out of school' youths in Guyana are achieving at low to moderate level of functional literacy. They also noted that there is a significant relationship between achievement in functional literacy and the level of education attained. The study found that students who did the Community High School programme showed the lowest level of achievement. This findings support the perception of employers, and the disenchantment of the public. The Community High School programme was a major attempt at making secondary education relevant to the development of Guyana. From the above discussion, it can be surmised, that this programme was not a success.

The government recognized that a high rate of functional illiteracy can impact negatively on the development of a country. To reverse the high rate of functional illiteracy among the out of school youths, the government has decided to remove dualism at the secondary level (State Paper on Education 1995). Embedded in this removal of dualism is the idea of transforming the Community High School programme to that of a General Secondary school programme. The programme of the Community High Schools and the Tops of Primary Schools would become a five-year programme, with the first year concentrating on remedial work in English Language and Mathematics.

The aims of this emphasis on secondary education as expressed in the (1995, p.22) Document, were:

> ...to produce graduates who are scientifically technologically and artistically literate, who have the capacity for critical thought and who can make intelligent use of knowledge acquired in the classroom, and in research in the solution of problems.

According to the document, some of the strategies to achieve these aims were to:

- Unify and restructure secondary education in order to improve the quality of education offered at this level.
- Design a curriculum with a core and foundation components for secondary education that would produce a graduate who is scientifically, technologically and artistically literate.
- Improve the working conditions of teachers; and the quality of the teaching, learning environment of secondary schools.

The Secondary School Reform project was introduced in 1996 to improve the quality of education offered in lower secondary schools and thus reverse the high rate of functional illiteracy.

THE SECONDARY SCHOOL REFORM PROJECT

The Secondary School Reform Project (SSRP) is a multiphase secondary education reform programme aimed to "...improve the quality, relevance, equity and efficiency of secondary education in Guyana..." (Hunte, 1997, p. 6). It was introduced in its pilot phase to twelve schools spanning the types which deliver a secondary programme. Through this project which lasted for seven years, it was hoped that all secondary age students would be provided with an effective and relevant basic education irrespective of the type of secondary school they are attending. With this in mind, the pilot schools consisted of two (2) General secondary schools, seven (7) Community High schools and three (3) Primary tops (Primary Schools with Secondary Departments). These schools were located in Regions Two, Three, Four, Five, Six, Ten, and Georgetown. According to Hunte (op cit) the key objective of the project is to ... facilitate the raising of the level of educational achievement from students of all abilities, aptitudes and interests at the end of their period of compulsory schooling.

Since the achievement of this general objective demanded that other improvements be in place, the SSRP focused on three major inter-retailed components:

- Education Program Quality
- School Environment
- National and Regional Institutional Strengthening

EDUCATION PROGRAM QUALITY

Hunte (op cit) stated that this component's two major objectives were to:

(i)   Introduce decentralised, cost – effective, sustainable, integrated school – based quality improvements

(ii) Develop, test and implement new and more relevant multi-level common curricula in the four core subjects (English Language, Mathematics, Science, Social Studies) and Reading

This component facilitated the updating of the content and approaches to teaching and learning to make them consistent with on going changes in the education system and the development, validation and distribution of a common curriculum and teachers' guides for each of the four core areas and Reading for the first three levels of secondary schools. Further, this component which initiated the national assessment of student attainment at the end of Third Form for English Language and Mathematics in 2001, has influenced the administration of a compulsory battery of tests annually for the core subjects –English Language, Mathematics, Social Studies and Science.

It was widely recognized that the teachers and administrators of a school were the ones who could make a reform a success. Lee (1995) attribute a committed group of teachers, a supportive administration and adequate resources, as factors which contribute to successful education reform implementation of any project. The subject teachers involved in the reform project were exposed to content, methodology and assessment workshops, conducted during the vacation periods. Workshops were also held for. Head teachers, Deputy Head teachers, Seniors and Heads of Departments. They were exposed to the tenets of Curriculum Management, Management and Supervision, Participatory Management and Supervision, and the Management of Change. Administrators and teachers in pilot schools also benefited from technical support and on the job training by the supervision team members of the project. Support was given in the core areas and reading and in school management. The aim of all the various training was to improve teacher's competence. This training was in-keeping with one of Beuchler's (2000) approaches to the creation of successful schools: that is the development of building high quality professional staff. Behind this approach is the thinking that since teachers are a critical ingredient in any reform process, it is assumed that the teachers' role will change. In this new role, teachers are seen as facilitators of learning rather than imparters of knowledge, dictating what happens in the classroom.

Among the systems implemented for students were different types of field exercises/activities, the provision of text books to encourage private work at home, and upgrading of libraries. The general aim through all this was to get them more interested in school and the activities therein and thus improving attendance and retention rates.

SCHOOL ENVIRONMENT

The School Environment, component was designed to improve the learning environment of schools through the rehabilitation of various physical facilities which were considered hindrances to the learning process Hunte (1997), asserted that the project facilitated the building, rehabilitation, or renovation, extension of buildings, construction of multipurpose laboratories and acquisition of furniture for pilot and non-pilot schools.

NATIONAL AND REGIONAL INSTITUTIONAL STRENGTHENING

The SSRP in its quest to strengthen and support the education system provided, training for education officials to strengthen their budgetary practice, school-based management systems, effective leadership, use of office technology so as to better coordinate the activities of the project. It was hoped that the overall effectiveness of education administration would improve, thus enhancing the ability of these officials to design, plan for, and implement sustainable education reforms.

The achievement of the key objective greatly depended on the achievement of several specific objectives which could only be achieved through the completion of the activities, given under the various components. The specific objectives were:

• Test the developments of the reform in twelve (12) pilot schools

- Develop curriculum materials and a National Third Form Examination in the core subjects
- Identify and provide the pilot schools with relevant teaching and learning materials
- Train teachers and education officers to improve the delivery of education
- Establish standards for the design, development and maintenance of physical facilities
- Rehabilitate and extend all pilot schools and repair twenty (20) non-pilot schools
- Provide pilot schools with financial resources and incentives for school improvement
- Develop a school information system
- Empower parents/guardians and their communities to participate in the improvement of their schools

In keeping with the key objective of SSRP, those schools which started in the project as Community High Schools and Tops of Primary Schools were no longer referred to as such. They were established as discrete Secondary Schools. The project then had twelve 'secondary schools'. In addition to this, the children in the converted secondary schools were given new badges and new uniforms thus helping them to realize that they were starting on a new era in education – that of being exposed to quality education through the use of the same curricula as the general secondary schools in Guyana. Through all of this, it was hoped that the attendance rate of teachers and students would improve, since it was said that the teachers and students at these schools (before they were concerted to General Secondary Schools) were more often absent than the teachers and the students attached to the other secondary schools. It was also stated that the drop out rates at Community High Schools and Tops of Primary Schools were usually higher than in other secondary schools.

Several indicators are taken into consideration when doing an evaluation. Several were used to monitor and measure success in the SSRP. Each component had its own indicators. The writer is cognizant of the fact that all components of SSRP were considered important and that all components were carefully prepared so that they could support the achievement of the key objective of raising the attainment level of students. The writer nevertheless examined only the indicators which were used to determine the success of SSRP for the Education Program Quality component since at the time of writing detailed information on the other components were not readily available.

The indicators under the Education Program Quality were placed into three groups. These were Input, Output, and Process Based Indicators.

The Input based indicators were used to assess whether the materials necessary for use in the pilot schools were delivered and were used as expected. Some of these indicators enquired whether Curriculum Guides, Teachers' Guides, Text books, and non-text learning materials were distributed to Pilot schools.

Indicators were also used to determine if teachers were trained in Content and Methodology for core subjects and Reading and whether school administrators were trained in school management, leadership and school improvement plan development.

Having the materials and acquiring the training to use the materials do not always mean that they are being used, thus Process Based Indicators were prepared to assess the use of the materials.

The Process Based Indicators were used while monitoring schools to ensure that the Inputs were being used as recommended or to improve learning. Some of these were used to determine whether teachers were using Curriculum Guides and Teachers' Guides for Planning Curriculum and whether supervisory visits by Education Officers/Supervisors were made to Pilot Schools.

Output, Based Indicators on the other hand, were used to monitor the success of the Input and Process Based Indicators. Some of these indicators were used to determine if the Teachers of the pilot schools were using non-text materials and equipment for curriculum delivery. They were also used to determine whether the percentage average student attendance, the percentage average student drop–out rate for (a) Grade Seven, (b) Grade Eight, (c) Grade Nine, and the percentage average student performance at the National Third Form

Examination for (a) English Language, (b) Mathematics were improving.

Once the results of the Output based Indicators were favourable, then one can presuppose that the results for each of the pilot schools at the National Third Form Examination, would be favourable. This chapter is mainly concerned with those indicators which were used to monitor the performance at the National Third Form Examination.

SUCCESS / FAILURE OF SSRP – EDUCATION PROGRAM QUALITY

By the end of the Project (August 2004), a variety of curriculum materials were in schools. Some of these were Curriculum Guides and Teachers' Guides for Social Studies, Science, English Language, Reading, and Mathematics, Expressive Arts, Industrial Technology (Engineering, Technology, Building Technology, Electrical Technology, Mechanical Engineering Technology and Technical Drawing) and Agricultural Science. These were all done for Grades / Levels 7, 8 and 9. A Careers Education: Handbook for Secondary Teachers was also prepared.

By the end of the project, the success which was revealed during the progress evaluation was not evident in all areas. Hunte (2003, p.3), in referring to the results of the pilot schools at the Caribbean Secondary Education Certificate Examination notes that the 2001 – 2003 CSEC results have shown that the performances of some of the students placed at the seven (7) Community High Schools and three (3) Primary Tops were just as good or a little better than the average performance of students attending the General secondary schools. He however notes, on the other hand, that the high standards achieved when the SSRP supervisors made regular visits to the pilot schools, to assist with professional developments, had dropped. Smith (2003, p. 1) reveals after final visits made to the pilot schools that some headteachers had failed to insist that their teachers use the learning materials and equipment given to their schools. This drop in standard was expected to some extent since the writer, like Simyle (1995), and Sparks (1995), feels that professional development should be continuous and closely monitored. The visits had stopped almost two years before the end of the project.

In an independent evaluation of the English Language and Mathematics attainments of the Secondary Schools Reform Project, Phoenix (2004) found that the SSRP students had lower perception of the programme than non-SSRP students. This finding was in keeping with public perception. The study also found that the project was unable to raise the academic attainment levels of the students in its pilot schools when compared to non-pilot schools. It should be noted that two general secondary schools were among the group of SSRP schools evaluated.

A thirty-item perception questionnaire, a forty-item paper and pencil Multiple Choice Test and the National Third Form Examinations results for Mathematics and English Language for 2001, 2002 and 2003, were used in the evaluation.

The aim of SSRP was to develop measures to improve secondary education and to test these measures in twelve schools in six of the ten Administrative Regions in Guyana. It could be argued that the project enjoyed some measure of success, if even it was only evident during the monitoring stage. Based on this, certain policy decisions to improve secondary education in Guyana were made. Some were even made before the end of the project. These decisions/ implications will now be identified and discussed.

POLICY IMPLICATIONS EMITTING FROM THE EVALUATION OF SSRP.

1. UNIFICATION OF THE MANAGEMENT OF SECONDARY EDUCATION.

Prior to 1997, there was an Assistant Chief Education Officer responsible for community high schools and there was an Officer responsible for general secondary schools. There is now one Officer for all secondary schools including community high Schools. To assist the Assistant Chief Education Officer (Secondary) are a Senior Education Officer (Arts) Senior Education Officer Mathematics/Science and a Senior Education Officer (Work Study).

COMMON CURRICULUM GUIDES FOR
SECONDARY SCHOOLS.

The Ministry of Education has taken a decision to remove inequalities in secondary education. In light of this, the Ministry has decided that students will cover a common curriculum for the first three years of secondary education. This initiative was done with the SSRP Pilot schools. The policy makers are cognizant of the fact that all secondary school students do not start secondary education with the same ability. Some of them obtained scores that were far below the national mean for each subject at the Secondary Schools Entrance Examination while others did exceptionally well – obtaining more than eighty percent of the marks for each subject. In light of this, the Ministry in its 'Strategic Plan' for2003-2007, (2003, p.10), reiterates that students will cover a common curriculum for the first three years of secondary school with extra support in Mathematics and English Language for weaker students. With a common curriculum the path towards obtaining Universal Secondary Education in Guyana has been cleared.

Universal Secondary Education is one of the legacies of the Secondary Schools Reform Project. With Universal Secondary Education the Ministry is committed to changing all Community High Schools to secondary institutions. With this change, some Tops of Primary Schools will also be changed to Secondary institutions while others would become discrete primary schools.

With the move towards Universal Secondary Education, it was decided that all students receiving a secondary education should be given the opportunity to write the Caribbean Secondary Education Certificate (CSEC) Examination. Prior to the implementation of the Secondary School Reform Project, an extremely small number of students at a few Community High Schools were given the opportunity to write subjects at (CSEC).

The Secondary School Reform Project has reversed this trend. Now many children at these lower secondary schools are writing four or more subjects. This is definitely a boast in the education system.

COMPULSORY WRITING OF THE NATIONAL GRADE NINE EXAMINATION.

The National Grade Nine Examination was piloted by the SSRP in 2001 under the name of the National Third Form Examination Mathematics and English Language was done. In 2002 the other core subjects Social Studies and Science were added, thus bringing the cadre of subjects to four. These subjects all have a Project (School Based Assessment) attached to them. Each Project is worth 25% of the total marks. This component of the examination gears students towards the preparation of School Based Assessments for the Caribbean Secondary Education Certificate.

The Ministry of Education has made this examination compulsory for all Grade Nine Students. The results of this examination are now used to identify the students whose fees for writing the Caribbean Secondary Education Certificate examination should be subsidised.

Emanating from this policy decision too is that all students from Grades Seven to Nine must do Science. This subject was optional in community high schools prior to 2001.

PREPARATION OF NATIONAL EXAMINATIONS FOR GRADES SEVEN AND EIGHT BY EACH REGION

Another Policy decision taken is that all education departments must prepare a National Grade Seven and a National Grade Eight Examinations for the core areas along with Projects for each subject. Under the Secondary Schools Reform Project, examinations were prepared for students at Grades 7, 8 and 9. These examinations were open to other schools who wanted to use the examinations instead of preparing examinations for their schools for these Grades. Examinations were done for Mathematics, Science, Social Studies and English Language. After the beginning of the National Grade Nine Examination, the SSRP only did examinations for Grades 7 and 8.

The regions began the preparations of the examinations in 2003 with guidelines and a schedule of activities prepared by SSRP for the conduct of the examinations. These examinations are being used annually in the regions.

PREPARATION OF SCHOOL IMPROVEMENT PLAN (SIP)

Under the SSRP, pilot schools were required to prepare a School Improvement Plan (SIP). This plan took into consideration School Management, Curriculum Delivery, Relationship with Parents/ Guardians, Student Welfare, Student Performance, Maintenance of the School Environment and Community Alliance. This School Improvement Plan was prepared in collaboration with parents teachers and other stake holders. All schools are now required to prepare and use a School Improvement Plan. Many researchers have attested to the fact that parental involvement has a positive influence on student achievement (Keith & Keith, 1993; Horn & Chen, 1998). Perry (1993) also supports this view since he found that the bigger obstacle to successful school reform was parental non- involvement or limited involvement. Once parents are involved in the SIP, then the rewards in terms of the effective delivery of education should be encouraging. Five major implications resulting from the evaluation of SSRP were discussed above.

These implications can be termed very important ones which the Ministry of Education feels will work towards the improvement of secondary education and thus student achievement. These implications suggest that much faith was put on the results of SSRP for the Ministry of Education and its policy markers to want to duplicate some aspects of the project. If the evaluation on which these implications are based were not accurate then the secondary education system can be jeopardized. It is hoped that clear guideline were used in the evaluation of SSRP and that objective results of the evaluation were obtained. After all, the future of secondary education is at stake and so too is the development of Guyana.

REFERENCES

Bisnauth, D. (1997, September). The focus is to raise the levels of performance of weak schools, not to lower the standards of better schools. *The Reformer*, 1, Guyana.

Bisnauth, D. (1999, September). Much rides on the SSRP. *The Reformer*, 1, Guyana.

Bovell, J. (1976). *The Community High School*. Ministry of Education and Cultural Development. Guyana Unpublished.

Buechler, M. (Ed.). (2000). *Closing the achievement GAP at the secondary level through comprehensive school reform*. Georgia: Northwest Regional Educational Laboratory.

De Young, A.J., & Balzhan, S. (1996). Issues in post-Soviet secondary school reform: The Case of Kazakstan. Rural Education and Small Schools. *International Journal of Educational Reform, 6*(4), 441-54.

De Young, A.J.,& Valyayeva, G.(1997). Post-Soviet secondary school reform in Kazakstan: the view of 149 classroom teachers. *Central Asia Monitor, 3.*

Farrant, J.S. (1980). *Principles and Practice of Education*. London, U.K: Longman Group.

Hunte, K. (1997, September). Questions and answers. *The Reformer*, 6-8, Guyana.

Hunte, K. (2004, July). Quality assurance, the challenge for the sustainable development of secondary education. *The Reformer*, 3-6, Guyana.

Jennings, Z., Kellman, W., Clarke, C., & Joseph, V (1995). *Functional Literacy Survey of out-of-school youth in Guyana*. Georgetown: University of Guyana.

Lee, V. E. (1995). Another look at high school restructuring: More evidence that it improves student achievement and more insights into why. *Issues in Restructuring Schools*, 9,1-10

Ministry of Education, (2003). *Strategic Plan- 2003-2007 Government of Guyana 2003* Guyana: Ministry of Education.

Ministry of Education, (1998). *Secondary School Reform Project 1999 Examination: Analytical Report*. Guyana: Ministry of Education.

Ministry of Education and Cultural Development, Guyana (1995*). An Education Policy and Five – year Development Plan for Guyana: providing education in an environment of economic crisis and political change.* Guyana Ministry of education and Cultural Development.

Moore, J., & Barab, S. (2002). The Inquiry Learning Forum: A Community of Practice Approach to Online Professional Development. *Tech Trends, 46*(3), 44-49

Murray, W. (2003, September 19). *PNC/R not impressed with CXC results.* Guyana Chronicle.

Osei, G.M. (2003). Issues arising from an examination of the Junior Secondary School Reform of 1987 in Ghana. *Educational Studies, 29*(2-3), 141-177.

Paul, U. (1979). *A Follow-up Study of the Community High School graduates: Development of a tracer system*. Guyana: Ministry of Education, social Development and Culture.

Perry, C. (In press). *BEAMS Transition Report*. Guyana: Ministry of Education

Perry, N. (1993). School reform: Big pain, little gain. *Fortune, 128*, November 29, 130-138.

Phoenix, C. (2004). *An Independent evaluation of the comparative English Language and Mathematics attainments of the Secondary Schools Reform Programme in Guyana*. (Masters Thesis). University of Guyana.

Sinylie, M. (1993). Teacher learning in the workplace: Implications for school reform. In T. Guskey & M. Huberman (Eds.), *Professional development in education: New paradigms and practices*. New York: Teachers College Press.

Smith, G. (2004, July).Editorial –Giving your students the best. *The Reformer*, 1, Guyana.

Sparks, D. (1995). A paradigm shift in professional development. *ERIC Review, 3*(3), 2-4.

CLAUDETTE PHOENIX

Chapter 6

RETHINKING THE FINANCING OF THE EDUCATION SYSTEM IN JAMAICA

DISRAELI M. HUTTON

ABSTRACT

The financing of the education system by government has been skewed toward pre-tertiary levels for the past two decades, and all indications are that this approach will be pursued with greater intensity in the future. The supporting evidence is revealed by the allocation of funding to the different levels of the education system and the articulated policy direction by senior officials of the Jamaican government. The purpose of this paper is to demonstrate the need for government to pursue a holistic approach to the funding of the education system as the country embarks on a process of transforming public education. In addition to its present commitment to tertiary and higher education, the government is advised to employ a policy of strategic apportioning of additional funding to support tertiary and higher education. This will involve targeted funding to critical areas of the tertiary and higher education system. Because of the important role tertiary and higher education play in the development of a country, one primary goal at this level is to increase significantly the number of students being trained from an age participation rate (APR) of less that 20% to the recommended 50% which obtains in developed countries and is being pursued by many developing countries with the same aspirations like Jamaica. Having one of the lowest per capita incomes among the countries of CARICOM, coupled with the fact that an increase in the APR for tertiary and higher education will depend largely on the recruitment of students from the social classes least able to fund higher education, it is necessary for government to continue to play the leading role in funding tertiary and higher education. Like all other developing countries, government is faced with commitments far in excess of its capabilities. The policy of strategic apportioning of funding or the targeting of definite areas for supporting tertiary and higher education will establish a specific role for government. Among the crucial areas for government's intervention are the (a) renovation and expansion of the physical plants, (b) upgrading of the research capabilities of tertiary and higher educational institutions in terms of their technical and scientific resources, and (c) strengthening the human resources capacity at the level of their academic and research leadership.

OVERVIEW OF THE EDUCATION FUNDING ISSUE

A holistic approach to the funding of the education system is one alternative that should be considered, as the country seeks to grapple with the multiplicity of deficiencies facing each level of the system. This will be a significant challenge to Jamaica in light of the fact that "roughly half of government expenditure are devoted to interest payments and high primary budget surpluses are required to stop debt from growing and presenting negative debt dynamics" (IDB, 2006, p. 5). Despite the crippling problems affecting each level the education, there is a deliberate approach by government to separate the financing of tertiary and higher education from that of early childhood, primary and secondary education. This position is advanced on the basis that with the limited resources available to government, increased funding should not be provided for tertiary and higher education because of the following reasons: (a) government has other commitments and responsibilities to the society, (b) the funding of tertiary and higher education should be shared with private sources, (c) the greatest problems of performance of the education system is rooted at the early childhood, primary and secondary levels, and (d) the resources made available to the education system are not being used efficiently and effectively at the tertiary and university levels.

The finance constraints facing the Jamaica economy is also the experience of many other developing countries. The UNESCO (2003) report on trends and development in higher education, pointed out that "education is just one of the sectors that seek funds from the state budget. The needs of other public services are growing, economic growth is slowing down or stagnant in many countries and public funding is scarce" (p. 10). While there may be validity to the fact that the weak economic situation of many developing countries intensifies the competition for scarce resources among public sector entities, the financing of the whole education system must be considered as a national priority because of its importance to the development of the country.

WHAT IS GOVERNMENT'S CURRENT THINKING ON THE FINANCING OF HIGHER EDUCATION?

The government is gradually withdrawing from what many feel is its primary role of funding tertiary and higher education. Davies (2005), Jamaica's Minister of Finance and Planning, indicated that the government cannot continue to play the hegemonic role in the funding of higher education and steps should be taken to target alternative sources in addition to what the state is able to provide. Davies (2005) recommended that the financial sector (needs) to design instruments which are specifically geared toward promoting long-term savings to meet these obligations. Parents need to engage in long-term planning to meet these obligations and (educational) institutions will need to identify new sources of funding" (P. 125).

In 2005, the policy direction is further clarified by the Minister of Education (Henry-Wilson) who, in addressing the issue of government expenditure on higher education, said that "these high subsidies to public tertiary institutions are not only an inefficient educational investment but also regressive social spending. Indeed, it is arguable that higher education should not have the highest priority claim in public resources for education" (p. 9). This perspective is not limited to Jamaica. The UNESCO (2003) report pointed out that "difficult policy choices have to be made between providing of higher education expansion and giving basic education the top priority that is required" (p. 10). However, the government cannot be ambivalent about its role and responsibilities related to tertiary education. Henry-Wilson also said that "the country needs to strike the right balance of resource allocation between all sectors of the education system, considering the relative social rates of return at each level as well as the complementarity which exists between the levels" (p. 9). This latter position clearly delineates the general approach which recognizes the critical importance of all levels of the education system. A balanced funding model must consider factors such as the (a) funding gap to be covered in order for each level of the education system to function at the required standard, (b) the role and responsibilities of all relevant stakeholders in the financing of tertiary education, (c) priorities that each level of the education system must address in order to realize the impact on personal and economic growth, and (d) government's definitive commitment as the central provider of funding for the education system.

WHAT IS THE PRESENT PATTERN IN FINANCING THE EDUCATION SYSTEM?

The funding of higher education by the government of Jamaica must be seen against the background that "public debt in March 2006 was approximately 132 per cent of GDP—a level that not only represents a threat to macroeconomic stability but also absorbs significant resources" (IDB 2006, p. 5). A review of both recurrent and capital expenditure on the education system for budget years 2003/04 to 2005/06 shows an overall increase in recurrent expenditure representing all levels of the education system for the four budget years. However, the capital expenditure is clearly skewed in favour of primary and secondary schools.

An examination of the capital expenditure as a percentage of recurrent expenditure between budget years 2002/3 and 2005/6, shows primary, secondary and tertiary as 8%, 7% and 1%, respectively (see Table I). Miller (2005) also confirmed the disparity in funding between tertiary education and primary and secondary education, which has been a pattern over the past two decades. An analysis of capital expenditure from budget Year 1975/76 and 2001/02, Miller (2005) pointed out that "99 per cent of that investment has gone to primary and secondary education and less than 1.0 per cent of that investment was made in tertiary education" (p. 100). Miller concludes that "the virtual absence of capital investment in tertiary education not only reflects government policy and priorities but also those of donor agencies on which the government has relied" (p. 100).

148

Table I: Estimates of Expenditure by Functions and Programmes for each level of the Education System from 2002/2003-2005/2006 ($'000)

Budget Year	Type of Expenditure	Early Child-hood	Primary	Special Education	Secondary	Tertiary	Total
2002/03	Recurrent	1 092 536	7 638 417	293 993	7 821 639	4 040 801	20 887 386
	Capital	23 261	521 477	1000	97 330	20 932	664 000
	Total	1 115 797	8 159 894	294 993	7 918 969	4 061 733	21 551 386
2003/0 4	Recurrent	1 148 924	7 397 898	293 418	7 885 693	3 965 693	20 691 626
	Capital	64 890	540 996	1 000	224 010	25 000	855 896
	Total	1 213 814	7 938 894	294 418	8 109 703	3 990 693	21 547 522
2004/05	Recurrent	1 409 036	9 728 356	342 131	9 719 670	6 437 021	27 636 214
	Capital	51 535	276 735	1 000	175 139	25000	529 409
	Total	1 460 571	10 005 091	343 131	9 894 809	6 462 021	28 165 623
2005/06	Recurrent	1 480 883	11 692 830	350287	10485732	6857300	30 867 032
	Capital	428 599	1 433 016	1 000	1 931 429	50 000	3 844 044
	Total	1 909 482	13 125 846	351 287	12 417 161	6 907 300	34 711 076
Total	Recurrent	5 131 379	36 457 501	1 279 829	35 912 734	21 300 815	100 082 258
	Capital	568 285	2 772 194	4 000	2 427 908	120 932	5 893 319
Ratio: Capital to Recurrent Expenditure		11%	7.60%	0.31	6.80%	0.57%	5.9%

(Compiled from the PIOJ Social and Economic Survey Reports—2003 to 2005)

But the decline in government expenditure is not limited to the capital side. James and Williams (2005) indicated that "overall, there was a steady and substantial decline in the share of government spending in the overall national effort from about 93.2 per cent in 1991 to about 79 per cent in 2001" (p. 167). This means that although there was clearly an overall increase in expenditure on higher education between 2002/03 and 2005/06, the fact is that real erosion in expenditure occurred between 1991 and 2001 which would have retarded any effort to expand or upgrade higher education during the present period.

WHAT IS THE SIGNIFICANCE OF PRE-TERTIARY EDUCATION?

According to the UNESCO (1997) report on sustainable development "basic education provides the foundation for all future education and learning. Basic education is aimed at all goals of education: learning to learn, to do, to be . . . and to live together with others (p. 22). Jamaica has achieved universal education at the primary level with over 97% of the age cohort enrolled in schools. This achievement is consistent with UNESCO's global target for basic education, and it represents an important achievement for the education system; however, the issue of the overall quality is of significant concern. The Jamaica Five Year Development Plan (1990) pointed out that "attendance rates of primary and all age schools were 72 and 65 per cent, respectively. This national figure obscures the fact that, in some deep rural areas, attendance rates were as low as 50 per cent" (p. 20). Commenting on the conditions of the public school system, which include primary, all age and secondary schools, KPMG Report (1998) indicated that the improvement of basic standards was a central task that must be carried out in order to improve the performance of schools. The Task Force on Educational Reform (2004) pointed out that the situation has gotten worse since the publication of the KPMG Report.

Currently, 50% of schools (are) in need of major repairs. In addition, we understand that there is inadequate classroom space to allow for different teaching options such as mixed ability grouping, as well as inadequate staff rooms, administrative office space. . . . There is also inadequate ventilation and lighting, water supply, and sanitary facilities in several schools. (p. 60)

At present, the public education system is facing numerous challenges. Any failure to take corrective measures will impact all other levels of the education system, including higher education. As the UNESCO (2005b) report on primary education for all children stated "it is imperative that primary education remains high on the global agenda if education for all is to be achieved. Its importance for social and economic development makes it a basic right for every child" (p. 9). The financing issue for government, therefore, remains a crucial one, and its present posture to focus its energy and effort on primary and secondary education seems justifiable. However, as argued later, the financing of higher education is of no less importance. The interrelatedness and interdependency of both pre-tertiary education and tertiary and higher education provide the basis for government funding strategy to be holistic.

WHAT IS THE SIGNIFICANCE OF TERTIARY AND HIGHER EDUCATION?

Tertiary and higher education play a crucial role in many areas of the Jamaican economy. Clarke (2005) indicated that "one of the most fundamental aspects of the mission of tertiary education should be its participation in the development and improvement of education at the other levels of the education system" (p. 51). In elaborating on the point Clarke said that the improvement is not limited to the training of teachers but it also has an impact on the work being carried out in early childhood, primary and secondary education. The role of higher education is further highlighted by the fact that of the teachers who now work in the school system, "only 20% have a university degree as well as a trained teacher diploma" (Task Force Report, 2004, p. 21). The pool of teachers have to be increased so as to meet the requirements of transformed public education system, and those teachers already in the system have to be upgraded to meet the qualification requirement for teaching. So the upgrading of education system will depend significantly on the ability of the tertiary and higher education facilities to provide training to raise the technical and instructional skills of the teaching force.

Broadly speaking, higher education should also provide the technical and professional cadre for development. The UNESCO (1998) report on the world declaration on higher education for the twenty-first century made the assessment that:

> Higher education has given ample proof of its viability over the centuries and of its ability to change and to induce change and progress in society. Owing to the scope and pace of change, society has become increasingly knowledge-based so that higher learning and research now act as essential components of cultural, socio-economic and environmentally sustainable development of individuals, communities and nations. (p. 2)

The declaration further indicated that "while the need for closer links between higher education and the world of work is important worldwide, it is particularly vital for the developing countries and especially the least developed countries, given their low level of economic development" (UNESCO 1998, p. 13). Thus, the nature of work has changed from an industrial based where the production of goods was the dominant output to an economy that is service and knowledge based in its orientation. This new dispensation requires training at the tertiary and higher education levels. The UNESCO (2002) report addressing the issue of financing education indicated that "the translation of increase access to schools into increased availability of human capital depends critically on participation in and successful completion of higher levels of education" (p. 10). Commenting on the role of higher education in a new mode of economic activities, the UNESCO (2004b) final report on the meeting of higher education partners stated that "large sections of the population need to acquire advanced levels of knowledge and skills. The workforce becomes increasingly a knowledge workforce, which needs more advanced training, and constant updating and retraining throughout life" (p. 6). The role of tertiary and higher education is unquestionable a central factor to the economic growth and development of the country.

WHO IS ACCESSING HIGHER EDUCATION IN JAMAICA?

The expansion of secondary education over the past 20 years has resulted in over 80% of the age cohort accessing secondary education in Jamaica. Logically, this means that for the first time in the history of Jamaica, the children of the poor and working classes are able to benefit from secondary education. While increased access does not translate automatically into quality as seen in the performance of the newly upgraded secondary schools in the CXC examination, a basis has been provided for this goal to be achieved (PIOJ 2005). Of greater concern at the present time, however, is the fact that even though access has been increased significantly, it is the privileged members of the society that are benefiting from the higher education, especially at the university level. Discussing the impact of the present funding practices by government, James and William (2005) said that while the revenue for government expenditure is provided by all the tax payers of the country, it was the children of the wealthiest who were accessing tertiary and higher education. In effect, this distortion has resulted in the transfer of income from the poorest in the society to fund the education of the children of the rich.

There are signs that the composition of persons accessing higher education is changing, but the speed and rate of change seem much too slow to have the dramatic impact necessary on the development of the country. Anderson and Devonish (2004) reporting on a study they conducted relating to diversity and change at the University of the West Indies (UWI) said that:

> In 1983, close to two-fifth (39.2 per cent) of UWI's intake from the urban area were drawn from communities that were ranked as middle class or higher. By 2003, this share had fallen to a quarter of all new admissions (24.8 per cent). Conversely, over this period the urban lower middle class expanded their representation from 40 per cent of admissions in 1983 to 51 percent by 2003. (p. 32).

This trend may be similar for the other higher educational institutions, but the fact is that coupled with limited enrolment levels in tertiary and higher education, the change is inadequate to raise enrolment to the level of the developed countries for sometime to come. The students of the poor and lower middle class are those least able to afford higher education, even though government pays 80% of the economic cost for tuition in Jamaica. Furthermore, many of those students from urban communities who are now accessing higher education represent the first generation from the poor and lower middle class families to go beyond secondary education. It would seem appropriate that government should provide the highest level of support to enhance the chances of success. In fact this is the best route to ensure that Jamaica will achieve APR in tertiary and higher education at the shortest possible time.

WHAT ARE THE ENROLMENT PATTERNS IN THE JAMAICAN EDUCATION SYSTEM?

The funding of the education system with a view to strengthen pre-university level education while dramatically expanding higher education will be informed by the (a) goals to be achieved by the whole education system, and (b) actual performance of the system. The performance gap must be addressed in the shortest period of time, if the country is to realize its potential. Specifically, for the tertiary and higher education system, the major priorities will include the (a) size of the relevant age cohort accessing tertiary and higher education, and (c) capacity of the system to accommodate increased numbers of students over a relatively short period of time. The enrolment element therefore becomes an important focus in order to determine the required strategies for appropriate intervention.

In 2005, the total number of students enrolled in the public and private education at the early childhood, primary, and secondary levels was 741 221, which represented an increase of 1.2 % over the previous year. There was universal enrolment at the early childhood and primary levels, which was 98% and 96%, respectively. The enrolment level in the secondary schools was at 84.8 per cent (PIOJ, 2005). However, at the tertiary and higher education level, only 20.70 per cent of that age cohort or an estimated 48 946 students were enrolled in these institutions (see Table II). The enrolment level, while better than several other developing countries is far below the 50% APR boasted by the developed countries. Commenting on some of the countries with

156

poor rate of enrolment at the tertiary level, UNESCO (2005a) pointed out that the "Age Participation Rate languishes below 10 per cent in India and 5 per cent in parts of Sub-Saharan Africa" (p .11)

Table II: Student Enrolment by Levels in the Private and Public Educational Institutions in Jamaica during 2005

Level of Institution	Number of Students Enrolled	Estimated Size of Cohort by Levels	Gross Enrolment Rates (%)	Per cent of Total Enrolment
Preprimary	137 867	141 113	97.7	18.6
Primary	286 853	299 117	95.9	38.7
Special Education	5 189	Not Available	Not Available	0.7
Secondary	220 884	260 476	84.8	29.8
Post Secondary	41 928	72 678	57.7	5.6
Tertiary & Higher Education	48 946	236 454	20.7	6.6
Total	741 221	1 009 838	73.4	100

(Compiled from the PIOJ Economic and Social Survey of 2005)

Note. The size of the age cohort generated for post secondary level students would be slightly less if the gross enrolment rate (GER) was given for the Special Education level. The GER for the post-secondary level students was extrapolated from the data provided.

The reason for this relatively low enrolment in Jamaica could be attributed to several factors. Firstly, the majority of students completing secondary school do not meet the matriculation requirements for tertiary institution, especially universities. PIOJ (2005) reported that "of the 28 867 school candidates who sit the CSEC in June 2005, approximately 4 812 or 17.0 per cent met the matriculation requirements with four or more subjects including mathematics and English language" (22.12). As pointed out in the IDB (2006) report, even if matriculation allowed for either Math or English being one of the subjects passed by candidates, only 13 298 or

46.1 per cent of the number who sat the examination (which is about 35.0 per cent of the Grade 11 enrolment) was successful.

Secondly, there is insufficient physical space availability to accommodate additional students. While tertiary institutions would be able to provide training for more students, the physical capacity is not available. The University of the West Indies, for example, has been unable "to meet the needs of the now 12,000 strong population" (UWI 2005, p. 17) and achieve the targeted expansion of over 23 000, substantially as a result of inadequate space. Thirdly, the low level of enrolment of males relative to females in most tertiary institutions has effectively reduced the pool available to expand tertiary education. The Economic and Social Survey, Jamaica (2004) indicated that from 40 selected tertiary institutions, 15,524 males and 34,852 females were enrolled. This represents 30.8% males and 69.20% females, respectively. While the trend of a greater proportion of girls than boys enrolled in the school system increases as you move from one level to the other, the dramatic reduction in the enrolment of males is most evident at the tertiary level of the education system. Fourth, the rising cost of higher education. Even though students are required to pay only 20% of the economic cost of their education, the fact is that the actual cost of education for each student far exceeds the economic cost. These additional costs include transportation, meals, rental, clothing, books, equipment and health care make the actual cost of education for a significant number of students unbearable.

The pattern of enrolment in higher education for a cross-section of countries provides a basis for critiquing the funding of the Jamaican education system. South Korea, which enjoyed the status of a developing country like Jamaica in 1960s, has now shown remarkable progress in the education system and in particular higher education. UNESCO (2004a) indicated that, "in the Republic of Korea, more than 95% of the age group reached the last level of secondary education and 80% of graduates continue their studies in short or long higher education. The quantitative experience of the education system can therefore be considered as almost finished, except in preprimary" (p. 15). Mora and Vidal (2000) commenting on the level of enrolment in Spain's Education system said that "in the last decade, the Spanish higher education system has become a mass system, with increasing proportions of people enrolling in higher education institutions. The gross enrolment quota for the 18-23 years old population is 41%, and the percent of new entrants in higher education among 18 years cohort is 55%" (p. 248)

The UNESCO (2004b) report, addressing the issue on a global scale, pointed out that "current estimates figures indicate that enrolment rates around 40 per cent to 50 per cent of relevant population group are needed in order to allow for a country to function well in a globalize, competitive world" (p. 7). The developed countries are clearly cognizant of this reality, and they have aggressively sought to develop higher education and research so they now have an average APR of 50 per cent

WHY SHOULD GOVERNMENT PLAY THE PRIMARY ROLE IN THE FUNDING OF HIGHER EDUCATION IN JAMAICA?

Miller (2005), based on a review of the recurrent and capital expenditures on tertiary education between 1975 and 2002, concluded that "what is clear from the data is that, at the same time that tertiary education needs to be the vanguard in making the country wealthy and globally competitive, tertiary education is faced with stagnation from the perspective of public resources allocated to education" (p. 102). With the implementation of the transformation of early childhood, primary and secondary sub-sectors of the education system over the next 10 years, there is little evidence that government will make any significant investment in tertiary education. In fact, the estimates in the Task Force on Educational Reform Report (2004) is that with the usual budget requirement for operating these sectors "an additional $219 billion is required over the next 10 years (an increase of 73% or approximately $22 billion increase per year), of which $58.7 billion is capital and $160.6 billion for (recurrent) expenditure" (p. 8)

Promoters of the view that the private sector should increase its role in the provision of higher education pre-suppose a level of income available for the majority of Jamaican people to purchase tertiary and higher education. A look at the countries which are sometimes used as reference points for where Jamaica needs to be in terms of economic development and education achievement reveal the significant difference

160

in economic development. For example, Table III shows that South Korea, New Zealand, Singapore and Ireland have a per capita income that is between 4 and 11 times greater than Jamaica's. For the developed countries such as the United States of America, Australia and England where the privatization of the education is encouraged by Government, their per capita income is excess of 1100% that of Jamaica's (World Bank, 2006). As related by UNESCO (2006) report on Commonwealth of Learning:

> Many countries are witnessing a major change in the role of nation-state in higher education, especially through the loss of its monopoly over higher education policy. This is cause for concern for those who feel that increasing commercialization of higher education will adversely affect social inclusion and the educational opportunities of the poor (p. 8)

Even when such a comparison is taken to the regional level, Jamaica still remains at a disadvantage. A comparison of the per capita income of Jamaica with a number of the CARICOM member states shows Jamaica falling at bottom, if Guyana is excluded from the group. Countries such as Trinidad, Antigua and Barbuda, and Barbados have a per capita income of between 200% and 300% higher than that of Jamaica (see Table III). Despite their apparent economic advantage, several of these countries including Barbados and Trinidad and Tobago are providing full funding for those accessing tertiary education at regional or local universities. The Jamaican Government should examine carefully the advantages gained by those countries which are continuing to play a leading role in funding tertiary and higher education.

The position that government should play the leading role in funding the education system is further strengthened by the fact that any significant expansion in the number of persons accessing higher education will naturally rely on the emerging pool of students whose economic background would make them less able to afford it. Despite the availability of the student loan facilities, the cost to access tertiary and higher education by poorest students will continue to be a major challenge. James and William (2004) indicated that the "SLB (Student Loan Bureau) has not been successful in targeting the eligible poor with sufficient accuracy and effectiveness to give them most of the available benefits and bring about significant changes in their relative access to tertiary education" (p. 173). The reality is that for many of these students it will be a choice between expenditure on higher education and basic necessities such as food, rent, clothing and equipment required for their studies.

This dire situation seems far from improving. In fact it seems to be worsening. From an international perspective, Jamaica along with the other Caribbean countries is falling behind regarding their per capita income in comparison with some of the other nations of the world as indicated in Table III.

Table III: Per Capita Income for Selected English Speaking Caribbean Countries and Four Countries with Higher Levels of Development which are used for Comparison when Discussing the Economic Potential of Jamaica.

Country	Per Capita Income 2003	Per Capita Income 2004	Ranking	Per Capita Income 2005	Ranking
Antigua & Barbuda	9 330	10 000	36	10 920	56
Trinidad	7 790	8 580	38	10 440	58
St. Kitts & Nevis	6 860	7 600	41	8 210	66
St. Vincent & the Grenadines	3 250	3 650	66	3 590	95
Jamaica	2 780	2 900	73	3 400	99
Guyana	890	990	118	1 010	147
Ireland	27 020	34 280	9	40 150	10
Singapore	21 410	24 220	24	27 490	29
New Zealand	15 530	20 310	26	25 960	31
South Korea	12 050	13 980	33	15 380	49
Barbados*	9 270	Not Available		Not Available	

(Compiled from Finfacts Ireland and World Bank Development Databases 2004 and 2005)

Note: * The per capita income figures were not provided for Barbados, but based on similar information provided by UNESCO reports, the per capita income would be in excess of US$10 000 per annum for 2005. Thus, Barbados would have the highest per capita income among the selected English Speaking Caribbean countries.

WHAT ROLE SHOULD THE KEY STAKEHOLDERS PLAY IN THE FUNDING OF HIGHER EDUCATION?

The UNESCO (2002) report indicated that "public funding of higher education which remains its major source in the majority of the countries of the world is under heavy constraints. Education is just one of the sectors that seeks funds from the state budget" (p.14). The hard reality of the challenges faced by tertiary and higher education in many developing countries closely reflects the experience of Jamaica as a developing country. This is also borne out by the fact that Government's support for higher education is declining based on the level of spending being provided on an annual basis and the increased demand in areas such as health and security. However, UNESCO (2003) indicated that "a large number of governments, particular in the European region, remained committed to free higher education. The introduction of fees in public institutions meet resistance on behalf of the academic community, the students in particular, and the general public" (p. 11)

There is general agreement that government alone cannot fund the cost of education, so there should be a clear mechanism which specifies government's proportion or level of funding for tertiary and higher education. This will enable tertiary and higher educational level institutions to plan their growth and maintenance more effectively, based on a negotiated funding formula which specifies the proportions of spending by government, institutions and other funding sources. The path that is created for tertiary and higher education in the next five to ten years will determine the extent the Jamaica will match up to those countries which have taken full advantage of a highly developed tertiary education system. A national consensus should drive this process. This would allow some of the key stakeholders including business to demonstrate their commitment to higher education.

Universities should be required to strengthen their source of funding based on a fee structure that is affordable for the majority of students. This approach is even more important when there are clear indicators that the composition of the University student population is changing from the children of the privileged to those of the poor and lower classes. This trend will intensify in the next decade. Addressing the approaches being taken by some countries the UNESCO (2004) report of the final meeting on higher education partners indicated that "in addition to tuition fees, institutions use a wide range of modalities to secure additional funds. They market their teaching, research and other services, rent their facilities, set-up commercial enterprises of their own, or engage in joint commercial ventures with the business sector" (p. 12). Jamaica is uniquely positioned to take full advantage of an overseas students market that could provide significant levels of revenue for tertiary education. There are many factors including culture, climate, history and location which could be the basis for attracting overseas students who can afford to pay the full economic cost for tuition.

The USA and other developed countries have systematically promoted their universities as the best for higher education, and in fact a large number of tertiary and higher educational institutions are sustained in part by attracting a significant proportion of international students. This will only be possible for Jamaica if the facilities are renovated and expanded and the quality of research and scholarship is improved. In addition, the redesign of unattractive and weak programmes and the introduction of new marketable ones will also go a far way in increasing the potential for tertiary and higher education to take full advantage of this opportunity.

The establishment of foundations and endowments is a fairly new phenomenon for the higher educational institutions in the Jamaican higher educational landscape. This option must be further cultivated over time. Organizations and individuals both locally and overseas should be targeted to participate in a scheme which will contribute ultimately to the development of the country. Full advantage must be taken of the wealthy, persons of good will along with companies that are willing to be identified with the history of tertiary educational institutions.

The SLB must play a vital role in this approach. The present trend where it is those who are most able to afford to pay for higher education are accessing student loans must be reversed. What is truly required is a loan policy that will allow those who meet the matriculation requirements for entry into higher education to access loan facilities without the draconian requirements. It is also obvious that there are those who see borrowing as burdensome and on that basis decide the government ought to fund wholly their education. This should never be entertained.

In addition to government strengthening and modernizing the loan policy of the SLB, the banks and other similar institutions should be encouraged to partner with the SLB thus expanding substantially the loan pool available to tertiary students. Loans for tuition alone will be inadequate because there are the other needs of the students which must also be facilitated. Students and parents also have a role to play in addressing the financing of the education of their children. Appropriate personal education saving/insurance schemes will be able to assist at least for those in the middle and upper classes.

The private sector has been providing scholarships, especially for persons whose academic performance has been outstanding. This programme also needs to be expanded. The provision of sums of monies for designated and non-designated programmes would also assist higher educational programmes to do more for their students. Further, the traditional summer employment should be expanded, thus giving students an opportunity to earn and provide some support for themselves while they pursue their education. In addition, other companies should be able to provide employment during the normal work day which will facilitate part-time training and education for some students. Businesses should in fact provide support for a greater number of employees who need advanced training in order to improve on their technical and administrative skills. The public sector has had study leave programmes for staff members to upgrade their qualifications. For education, up to 10% of the academic staff can be on study leave each year.

A COMPREHENSIVE APPROACH TO THE TRANSFORMATION OF THE EDUCATION SYSTEM

The Jamaican education system is at a crossroad. This may be the opportune time for government to provide leadership and implement a comprehensive plan to address the issue of financing the education system. Commenting on the initial work done in relation to the sector-wide transformation of the Jamaican education system, the UNESCO (2005a) report indicated that "together with the public sector modernisation strategy in progress, Jamaica has already embarked on the road to educational transformation, having several of the building blocks for a sector-wide approach already in place or under development" (p. 1) In addition, much can be learned from the approach that was taken to review the public education system in relation to (a) selection of stakeholders, (b) the broad participation of entities such as the church, business, trade union, school system, professional organizations among others, and (c) the country-wide and inclusive strategy employed to achieve consensus (Task Force on Education Report, 2004).

To provide further credence for a broad-based approach to this issue, the UNESCO (2004a) report on educational policies and strategies noted that the model adopted for the financing of education for all by many countries is (a) sector wide, (b) participative, and (c) there are demonstrable concerns for local needs. Reporting on a number of countries seeking to introduce a policy of education for all, UNESCO (2004a) outlined that "the approach adopted by all countries examined is more participatory and strives to involve different partners (inclusive of) ministries other that the Ministry of Education, central public agencies, external corporation and funding agencies, local communities, representatives of civil society, particularly the NGOs, and families" (p. 11). In fact, Jamaica has already positioned itself to commence this journey but the determination and commitment seem to be waning. The UNESCO (2005a) report stated that the financing of sector-wide educational transformation in Jamaica points the way toward a broad-based and inclusive strategy:

A sector-wide approach attempts to put together the gamut of objectives and strategically prioritise them against a full resource envelope that encompasses public, private, individual, domestic and external financial resources. Another large part of the basis for consensus has to do with the engagement in policy dialogue of all those with a stake in the educational system to bring about accountability throughout the system for the disbursed resources to those different stakeholders, be they in central government, in the decentralized administrative units or, indeed, in the schools and communities themselves. (p. 1)

Bringing together the representatives from the key stakeholders such as international funding agencies could commence the charting of the road to the transformation of the whole education system. At present the focus seems to be on public or pre-tertiary education system, which gives support to the view that an 'either' 'or' approach is being taken at the expense of tertiary and higher education.

A POLICY OF STRATEGIC APPORTIONING OF FINANCING BY GOVERNMENT

There is a general consensus that the three critical areas for intervention in the Jamaican economy are security, health and education. The strategic apportioning of resources would be necessary to address the most important areas for intervention among each of the three social services sectors of the Jamaican economy. This means that the government, through a process of national consensus, would identify targeted areas of each to achieve the greatest impact. The issue of priority therefore would not be among the three services sectors but instead the targeted areas within each of the service sectors.

For the education service sector, the 'either', 'or' approach by government represents a strategic choice of funding pre-university level education transformation over tertiary and higher education. This approach fails to consider the interdependency and interrelatedness of all the levels of the education system. If the country had a tertiary and higher education system

170

with the capacity to provide the technical and professional competencies to drive the productive sectors and renew itself, there would be little difficulty in focusing support at the other levels of the education system. However, there are serious deficiencies with only 20% of the age cohort who are going on to higher education. Further, even if the government is able to expand the number of person accessing tertiary and higher education "the developmental benefit of such public spending is substantially undermined by emigration of about 80 percent of graduates" (IBD 2006, p. 11). With the limitation of adequate resources to treat with all levels of the education system, government has to apply the concept of strategic apportioning in order to maintain some balance and move the whole education system ahead at the same time.

GOVERNMENT APPLYING THE STRATEGIC APPROACHING TO THE EDUCATION SYSTEM

There are three areas that tertiary and higher education have the greatest challenges. The first area is the renovation and expansion of the institutional plants. A number of the institutions at the tertiary level are over 100 years old, and they need significant renovation and expansion. But in addition to their ages, these institutions do not have the physical capacity to accommodate any significant increase in the number of persons accessing higher education. In fact the pre-tertiary levels of the education system are facing the same type of situation. A study completed in 2005 shows that there is a requirement for an additional 400,000 spaces to satisfy the Task Force on Education parameters for space in the public education system (Hutton, 2005, p.10). For the tertiary and higher educational level, Government needs to make an intervention to substantially upgrade and expand the physical plant with a view to increase access to higher education. While different modalities including distance and internet are being used, these by themselves will not be able to overcome the technical and professional skills requirements of the workforce, or increase significantly the age participation rate of those who access tertiary and higher education. This one-off approach to renovation and expansion of the plants should address the space and quality needs of the facilities for another 30 years or more. (Of course, an adequate maintenance programme must be implemented to guarantee that the quality and functionality of the plants are prolonged for the planned duration of the facilities.)

The second area of initiative for government is the need to strengthen the research capability of universities and colleges. In order for the universities to operate at the cutting edge level, their technical and scientific capabilities must be comparable to those of the developed countries. The tertiary level institutions and universities by themselves will not be able to achieve the necessary capabilities in the near future without direct government or government supported interventions. For the University of the West Indies, for example, the libraries have essentially fallen behind by more than 10-15 years in terms of its collection of journals, and text books. While this and similar institutions seek to utilize the modern technology and provide various electronic data-bases for books, journals and other information sources, these have proven inadequate. The facilities for experimentation including the laboratories which have a direct bearing on the development of the economy should be one of the focuses of government's intervention for renewal and expansion

The third area that government resources could make a significant impact is strategic academic staff support. While the recurrent cost will be a constant burden on government, a flexible strategy could be employed where the government pays premium salary for professors who have a track record in research and are able to attract a high level of funding for their areas of research. These persons will be recruited from across the world and rewarded based on their potential to move the universities firmly among the world-rated institutions of higher education. It would be expected that such a programme would continue to attract the support of government for 10 to 15 years. By then the Universities would have raised significantly their resource based and the funding of higher education of the students would be less challenging issue to address by the majority of Jamaican.

The Jamaican education system is faced with numerous challenges, especially in relation to funding at the personal and institutional level. In order to significantly increase the APR of those who access tertiary and higher education, the majority of students will be recruited from those who are least able to afford it. Government will therefore have to continue to play the leading role in funding the whole education system. Tertiary and higher education institutions, however, must become more creative in meeting the financial needs related to the targeted cost areas. Government on the other hand will also be required to fund areas that are crucial to maintain the tertiary and higher education at world class level.

REFERENCES

Anderson, P. & Devonish, J. (2004). *The University of the West Indies: Diversity and change* Paper presented to the Conference on Diversity in higher education in higher and tertiary education, Kunming, China

Clarke, S.A. (2005). Tertiary education in a changing world. In R. Holding & O. Burke (Eds.), *Revisiting tertiary education policy in Jamaica: Towards personal gain or public good* (pp.3-10). Kingston: Ian Randle Publishers.

Davies, O. (2005). Financing higher education: The government perspective. In R. Holding & O. Burke (Eds.), *Revisiting tertiary education policy in Jamaica: Towards personal gain or public good* (pp.3-10). Kingston: Ian Randle Publishers.

Finfacts Ireland (2005). Global income per capita. Retrieved November 16, 2006 from *www.finfacts.com/biz10/globalworldincomepercapita.htm*

Henry-Wilson, M. (2005). Towards a higher education for Jamaica: The government perspective. In R. Holding & O. Burke (Eds.), *Revisiting tertiary education policy in Jamaica: Towards personal gain or public good* (pp.3-10). Kingston: Ian Randle Publishers.

Hutton, D. M. (2005). *Space audit and rationalization study.* Report presented to the Advisory Board of the Task Force on Education, October 2005

IDB (2006) *Country strategy with Jamaica (2006 – 2009).* Washington, D.C: Inter-American Development Bank.

James, V., & Williams C. (2005) Financing higher education: Policy choices for Jamaica. In R. Holding & O. Burke (Eds.), *Revisiting tertiary education policy in Jamaica: Towards personal gain or public good* (pp.3-10). Kingston: Ian Randle Publishers.

KPMG (1998). Strategic performance review of the Ministry of Education and Culture. Kingston, Jamaica: KPMG

Mora, J. & Vidal, J. (2000). Adequate policies and untended effects in Spanish higher education. *Tertiary Education and Management, 6,* 247- 258

Miller, E. (2005). The University of the West Indies, Mona, and tertiary education in Jamaica. In R. Holding & O. Burke (Eds.), *Revisiting tertiary education policy in Jamaica: Towards personal gain or public good* (pp.3-10). Kingston: Ian Randle Publishers.

PIOJ (1990). *Five Year Development Plan (1990-1995).* Kingston: Planning Institute of Jamaica

PIOJ (2005). *Economic and social survey.* Kingston: Planning Institute of Jamaica

PIOJ (Various Years). *Economic and social survey.* Kingston: Planning Institute of Jamaica

Task Force on Educational Reform (2004). *A transformed education system report* (Revised Edition). Kingston: Jamaica Information Service

UNESCO (1997). *Educating for sustainable development: A trans-disciplinary vision for concerted action.*

UNESCO (1998). World declaration on higher education for the twenty-first century: vision and action and framework for priority action for change and development (Adopted by the World Conference on Higher Education). Paris: UNESCO

UNESCO (2002). *Financing education-investments and returns: Analysis of the world education indicators.* Paris: UNESCO Publishing

UNESCO (2003). *Synthesis report on trends and development in higher education since the world conference on higher education (1998-2003).* Paris: UNESCO

UNESCO (2004a). *Education policies and strategies 6: Implementing and financing education for all.* Paris, UNESCO.

UNESCO (2004b). *Final report on the meeting of higher education partners* (World Conference on Higher Education +5, UNESCO, Paris 23 – 25, June 2003). Paris: UNESCO

UNESCO (2004c). *Higher education in a global society:* UNESCO education position paper. Paris, UNESCO.

UNESCO (2005a). *Financing sector-wide educational transformation.* (Expert report on inter-ministerial dialogue retreat and next steps, October 25-29, 2005). Paris, UNESCO.

UNESCO (2005b). *Primary education for all children.* Paris: UNESCO

UNESCO (2006). *Higher education crossing borders: A guide to the implications of the General Agreement on Trade in Services (GATS) for cross-boarder education.* Paris: Division of Higher Education.

UWI (2005). *Strategic repositioning: An agenda for action.* Kingston: University of the West Indies

Wikipedia (2005). *The free encyclopedia.* Retrieved November 16, 2006 from https:/www.wikipedia.org/wiki/list_of_countries by:GPA_(PPP)_per capita

World Bank (2006). World development indicators database. Retrieved November 16, 2006 from *http:// siteresources.worldbank.org/DATASTATISTICS/ Resources/* GNIPC.pdf

DISRAELI M. HUTTON

SECTION 3.

SCHOOL IMPROVEMENT

CHAPTER 7.

Pages 181 - 212
Principals' and Teachers' Perceptions of Principals' Instructional Leadership Roles in Selected Primary Schools in Central Jamaica

Beverley Johnson
Principal, Jericho Primary School, St. Catherine, Jamaica.

& Austin Ezenne
Department of Educational Studies, University of the West Indies, Mona, Kingston, Jamaica.

CHAPTER 8.

Pages 213 - 246
Secondary School Principals' Perceptions of the Management and Curricular Roles of Librarians in Jamaican Schools

Myrtle Elaine Harris
Documentation Centre, School of Education,
University of the West Indies, Mona, Kingston, Jamaica.

CHAPTER 9.

Pages 247 - 268
Teachers' and Students' Perceptions of Vocational and Technical Education Programme Planning in Jamaican High Schools.

Earl Christian
Ministry of Education and Culture,
Kingston, Jamaica

& Austin Ezenne
Department of Educational Studies,
University of the West Indies, Mona, Kingston, Jamaica.

CHAPTER 10.

Pages 269 - 294
Charting the Education Transformation Path: Towards Models of Praxis for Teacher Development for School Improvement in Jamaica

Paulette Feraria
Department of Educational Studies,
University of the West Indies, Mona, Kingston, Jamaica.

Chapter 7

PRINCIPALS' AND TEACHERS' PERCEPTIONS OF PRINCIPALS' INSTRUCTIONAL LEADERSHIP ROLES IN SELECTED PRIMARY SCHOOLS IN CENTRAL JAMAICA

BEVERLEY JOHNSON &
AUSTIN EZENNE

ABSTRACT

This research was undertaken to investigate the perceptions of teachers and principals about the roles of principals in instructional leadership in primary schools in central Jamaica. The respondents were drawn from thirty-nine primary schools and consisted of thirty-eight principals and three hundred and thirty-two teachers.

Data pertaining to teachers' and principals' perceptions were obtained through the Teachers' Evaluation of Principals Questionnaire (TEPQ) and the Principals' Self Evaluation Questionnaire (PSEQ). Ten questions looked at the principals' roles in instructional leadership and the data were analysed using descriptive statistics to ascertain the mean scores, standard deviations and frequencies for each respondent groups in each domain.

The major findings of this research suggest that principals and teachers were not sharing similar views pertaining to the principals' roles in instructional leadership. Specifically, some teachers did not agree that principals were carrying out their roles fully in instructional leadership, but principals agreed that they were carrying out these roles. Principals must try harder to improve their performance in instructional leadership in order to improve the quality of teaching and learning in the schools.

INTRODUCTION

As schools grapple with the many challenges facing the education system, the role of the principal becomes very critical. The question that often arises is –why some students learn and achieve and others do not? The answer lies partially in the quality of the instructional leadership role of the principal. The US National Association of Elementary School Principals (2002) proposes that high standards for student achievement call for high standards of performance from the adults involved in the education process and suggests that principals must be leaders in improving instruction and student achievement.

Winter and Dunaway (1997) in their contribution assert that the job of the principal might be the most challenging in administrative position in public education as school reform initiatives mandate greater emphasis on instructional leadership. In addition, past research on effective principal leadership (Murphy 1990, Drake & Roe 1999) proposes that principals should be focussed primarily on school processes of instruction.

Despite this however, many principals spend most of their time focussing on the mundane and routine exercises and not enough time on the instructional component. Jacobs (2000) states that while conventional wisdom and educational research assert that instructional leadership correlates positively with quality teaching and learning, many principals to do not devote enough time to supervising this absolutely crucial dimension of schooling- the instructional dimension. Drake and Roe (1999) purport that the pressures from the state consciously or unconsciously pushed principals towards a managerial emphasis... but there is the need for instructional leadership and management to function in harmony once priorities and procedures are established. They further call for principals to return to the role of "principal teacher".

Murphy (1990) supports the supposedly demise of the principals' roles in instructional leadership by identifying several studies, one of which reports that elementary school principals spend less than 2% of their time attending to instructional leadership responsibilities. In Murphy's survey, only 17% of principals' time and 8% of the tasks they perform deal with academic matters.

The roles of principals in instructional leadership in Jamaica have not undergone significant study as in developed countries. However the shift in focus and the various reforms in education globally have had serious implications for Jamaican principals. The Jamaican <u>Code of Regulations</u> (1980) has clearly stated the duties of principals as they relate to instructional leadership. However, the extent to which principals carry out these roles is questionable. In addition, the term "instructional leadership" is a relatively new concept in our Jamaican context, even though the concept is steeped in the duties and responsibilities as set out by the Code. Terms like "chief executive officer" and "administrator" have been used to describe the role of the principal. These terms underscore the managerial function of the principal. However, the importance of instructional dimension cannot be overemphasised. Hence a study of the principals and teachers' perceptions of the principals' roles in instructional leadership is quite timely and necessary.

THEORETICAL FRAMEWORK

Principals, because of the very nature of their legitimate authority and function have been considered as central figures in the overall scheme of education. Hallinger and Heck (1996) and Smylie and Hart (1999) as cited in Youngs and King (2002), purport that principals affect student performance indirectly through their influence on the school organisation and instructional quality. The role of principals in instructional leadership therefore cannot be taken lightly. Instructional leadership is the heart of the instructional programme for it is the direct contact made and assistance given by principals to teachers so that the instructional programme of the school can meet the needs of the pupils it serves. Davies (1991) contends that instructional development is intimately concerned with worthy performance and represents a striving for excellence through enhanced opportunities. He goes on to say that instructional development has both a strong analytic and synthesis role as well as a reflective and evaluative one. The US Jefferson County Public Schools (2003) underscores the role of an instructional leader as one who:

- Understands the philosophy of standards-based education and leads the implementation of that philosophy in the school;
- Leads the community in the development of challenging performance standards for students in the development of fair and accurate assessment;
- Understands effective models of instruction and coaches effective classroom instructional practices.
- Manages and supervises an instructional programme that fosters success for all students regardless of gender, race or disability. (p.2)

Griffith (1999) cited research which concurred with these roles by suggesting that an effective principal sets clear goals, encourages teaching of the 'basics', monitors student progress, and is actively immersed in the daily activities of the school.

Embedded in these roles is the importance of the instructional programme as well as the instructor (the teacher). A principal in his or her role in instructional leadership has to be committed to collaborating and communicating with teachers in order to improve instruction and learning and be involved in continuous instructional programme.

The term "instructional leadership" therefore sums up the primary role of the principal in the quest for academic excellence in education. In essence, the instructional leader focuses on student learning and student success. The student learning is facilitated and supported by the direct assistance given to teachers which according to Blase and Blase (2002) is designed to help teachers improve instruction through classroom observations, feedback, and reflective dialogue.

PRE-CONFERENCING

Pre- conferencing known also as pre-observation conferencing according to Kosmoski (1997) in Beach and Reinhartz (2000), is the most important stage of clinical supervision which is integral to instructional leadership. The purpose of this step is for principals to establish the guidelines and procedures for supervision and must facilitate open and honest communication.

Goldhammer, Anderson and Krajewski (1993) cited in Beach and Reinhartz (2000) states that pre-conferencing serves to:

a) Confirm and nurture the relationship between supervisor and teacher,

b) Provide an opportunity for the teacher to present his/her lesson plan in its polished state,

c) Give the teacher the opportunity to mentally rehearse the lesson in discussing the proposed teaching-learning episode,

d) Give the teacher the opportunity to revise lesson based on the discussion with the supervisor, and

e) Secure the agreement on the reasons for the observation and protocol to be followed. (p.130)

In many cases this important function is not observed as classroom visits are often done to catch teachers off-guard. This practice is reminiscent of the confusion and ignorance regarding supervision as against evaluation. Gordon and Schneider (1991) provided a distinction between the two terms. They succinctly explained that evaluation is the process whereby the strengths and weaknesses of an individual or group are identified and defined, while supervision is a process designed to capitalise on the strengths and correct any weakness of the individual or group.

CLASSROOM OBSERVATION

Classroom observation, according to Goldhammer (1969) as cited in Beach and Reinhartz (2000), captures the realities of the lesson objectively and comprehensively enough to enable the teacher to reconstruct the lesson as validly as possible afterwards. Classroom observation is critical to teacher performance and ultimately student success. For it is the process by which supervisors collect information about teaching and learning with the view to improve instruction and student outcome. Consequently, the role of the principal in classroom observation is very important. Beach and Reinhartz (2000) purport however, that classroom observation must not be confused with summative evaluation. As an instructional leader the principal is called upon to be a visible presence, hence frequent classroom visits are expected and required. These visits may take the form of formal or informal observations that can help to reinforce effective teaching, note emerging problems, and monitor curriculum implementation. As principals in their supervisory role conduct classroom observations, Calebrese and Zepeda (1997) note, as cited in Beach and Reinhartz (2000), that they are providing a "baseline of data to assist teachers" (p.158).

According to Beach and Reinhartz (2000) conducting classroom observation is a complex process as various modes of observation, different methods of data collection and different treatments of analysis of data are employed. Consequently, principals have to be aware of the fact that classrooms are multidimensional, unpredictable and unique.

Informal classroom observations are powerful in enabling principals to observe teaching /

learning situation that is not staged. Very often when teachers know that principals will be making official class visits, they plan staged performances and generally do a good job. However, it is the informal observations that speak volumes and that often reveal a true picture. The US National Association of Elementary School Principals (2002) emphasised that observations, are not to catch teachers doing something wrong but to ensure that all students are meaningfully engaged and actively learning. This statement suggests the negative views teachers as well as principals may have of classroom observation. These negative views are linked to poor planning, anxiety experienced by the teacher, the difference in how teacher and principal perceive what has happened in the classroom and poor follow-up. However Gordon and Schneider (1991) noted that these negative factors could be corrected by the supervisors who make the experience positive, and not reject the classroom visitation as one of their supervisory alternatives.

Classroom observations are important to schools as they enable teachers to display good teaching as well as for principals to support good teaching. They also allow the teachers to become aware of areas that could be improved while at the same time allowing principals to develop this awareness. They are very useful tools in providing feedback to teachers about the quality of their teaching, curriculum problems, and about groups of students or individuals. Concurrently, they allow principals to give these feedbacks and to assess the effectiveness of the curriculum (Glatthorn 1990).

189

THE IMPORTANCE OF FEEDBACK

Beach and Reinhartz (2000), suggested that once classroom observation has been analyzed and translated in a form that can be presented to the teacher it sets the stage for post observation conference where the principal provides feedback. For Checkley (2000), feedback is a necessary element in institutionalising a redefinition of teaching and learning, and is critical in providing teachers with data for modification and adjustment of classroom instruction.

As important as feedback is, however, it remains one of the most problematic. It is expected that principals should employ collegial and non-judgemental approaches in this instructional conference, however, Glanz (1994), Sergiovanni (1998) described the impersonal, judgemental nature of supervision approaches during conferencing and its harmful effects on teachers. Consequently, St. Maurice (2002) called for instructional leaders to participate in disciplined self-study about their supervisory practices. Hill (1996) suggested that effective feedback should be characterised by clear motives, it should be specific, simple, descriptive, validating, owned, well-timed, accurate, solicited, understood and should involve sharing of information. She advised that a principal should be in the problem-solving interview mode where he /she is no longer a judge but a helper as the goal is to develop the employee to think constructively and feel increased sense of job satisfaction.

METHODOLOGY

The data used in this study were collected using two questionnaires, which gathered information from thirty nine (39) principals and three hundred and thirty-two (332) teachers from forty (40) primary schools randomly selected in central Jamaica regarding the principals' roles in instructional supervision. The questions sought to glean information about the principals and teachers' perception of the principals' roles in instructional leadership.

Two questionnaires were developed to gather the data, one for principals and one for teachers. They were entitled Principals Self Evaluation Questionnaire (**PSEQ**) and Teachers Evaluation of Principals Questionnaire (**TEPQ**).

The questionnaire employed a five- point Likert –type scale where respondents were asked to rate each item ranging from 1-5, 1= strongly disagree, 2= disagree, 3=neutral, 4= agree, and 5= strongly agree. 0 was used to represent missing values.

The instrument was tested for reliability using Cronbach Alpha (C-alpha). The items pertaining to Instructional Leadership had a C-alpha of .8303.This demonstrated that the items were correlated significantly as they need to be at least 0.75 to be acceptable.

The data was analysed using 'Descriptives' or descriptive statistics to summarise scores on the various items in each domain for teachers and principals to ascertain the mean, median and mode (measure of central tendency), and range, deviation and standard deviations (measures of variability). The mean was significant in determining whether or not the principals were perceived as functional in their roles in instructional leadership. A mean of four (4) or above would suggest that principals were functional in their roles while means below (4) suggest a need for improvement. The standard deviation showed the scatter of all the deviations about the mean scores from the sample population.

ANALYSIS OF DATA AND DISCUSSION OF RESULTS

The following table, Table 1, provides a summary of mean scores and standard deviations of the responses to the ten items in instructional development/ leadership. This presents a comprehensive and clear picture of the relationship between the scores from each respondent group.

RESEARCH QUESTION 1:

Do principals establish criteria for maintaining academic standards in the schools?

A descriptive data analysis of the teachers' scores (TEPQ) revealed that the mean score was 4.24 out of a possible 5. (A score of 4 or more means that respondents agree that this function is being carried out.) The teachers' mean score corroborated with the principals' scores (PSEQ) which revealed a mean score of 4.53 and implies that it is agreed by both groups of respondents that principals were establishing criteria for maintaining academic standards in school.

Table 1: Summary of Respondents Mean Scores and Deviations on Instructional Leadership

QUESTIONS	TEACHERS (TEPQ)			PRINCIPALS (PSEQ)		
	n	Mean Score	S.D.	n	Mean Score	S.D.
1. Establish criteria for maintaining academic standard	322	4.24	.941	38	4.53	.506
2. Monitor students' progress through periodic tests and exams	322	4.05	1.140	38	4.61	.887
3. Promote programmes for individual differences	322	3.53	1.228	38	4.00	1.115
4. Monitor procedures for students' reports	322	3.90	1.214	38	4.18	1.504
5. Hold pre-conferences prior to making classroom visits	322	2.96	1.301	38	2.87	1.119
6. Visit classrooms regularly to ensure that students are meaningfully engaged	322	3.43	1.233	38	4.00	.900
7. Hold post conferences to provide feedback after classroom visits	322	3.70	1.248	38	4.24	.943
8. Protect contact time to ensure major part is spent on teaching/learning activities	322	4.29	.863	38	4.63	.489
9. Co-ordinate timetable to maximise use of instructional materials to promote learning	322	4.00	1.102	38	4.53	1.133
10. Provide up-to-date teaching/learning materials	322	3.79	1.159	38	4.26	.724
AVERAGE		3.789			4.185	

However an examination of the standard deviations for both respondents (principals and teachers) revealed that the variances on the items or the measures of dispersion within these groups were fairly significant. The principals' standard deviation was .506 in comparison to the teachers' which was .941. This suggests that the distribution of the scores of teachers was wider or less homogeneous than that of the principals.

It has been established the introductory statements and review of literature that students are the whole purpose for schooling and as such, the maintenance of academic standards is steeped in the principals' roles in instructional leadership. The US National Association of Elementary School Principals (2002) proposes that high standards for student achievement call for high standards of performance from the adults involved in the education process and suggests that principals must be leaders in improving instruction and student achievement. It is therefore encouraging to note that both teachers and principals believe that principals are establishing criteria for academic standards.

RESEARCH QUESTION 2:

Do principals monitor students' progress through periodic tests and exams?

The mean score for this question on the teachers was 4.05. This did not corroborate with the mean score of the principals which was 4.61. However, the results indicated that both groups of respondents agreed that principals were functional in monitoring students' progress. Drake and Roe (1999) have identified this function as one of the ten functions or duties of the principal which has an instructional emphasis. It is therefore noteworthy that principals are carrying out this role.

RESEARCH QUESTION 3:

Do principals promote programmes to meet students' individual differences?

The mean score of the teachers' scores on the Teachers Evaluation of Principals Questionnaire (TEPQ) was 3.53 while that of the Principals Self Evaluation questionnaire (PESQ) was 4, which suggest that there is no corroboration between the responses even though the variances on items within each group are not significantly different. (Table 2)

Table 2: Showing Frequency, Percent, Mean and S.D. for 'Promoting Programmes for Individual Differences'

	Frequency		Percent		Mean Scores		Standard Deviations	
	Teacher	Principal.	Teacher	Principal	Teacher	Principal.	Teacher	Principal.
Valid 0	10	2	3.0	5.3	3.53	4.00	1.228	1.115
1	17	0	5.1	0				
2	28	0	8.4	0				
3	79	3	23.8	7.9				
4	129	22	38.9	57.9				
5	69	11	20.8	28.9				
Total	332	38	100.0	100.0				

Examination of the frequencies and percent showed that only 59.7% of the teachers strongly agreed or agreed that principals were promoting programmes to meet pupils' individual differences. In contrast, 86.8% of the principals strongly agreed or agreed that they were doing so. These scores underscore the discrepancies that have been revealed so far between the teachers' perceptions about the principals' instruction roles and that of the principals themselves, meaning that the teachers and principals are not sharing similar opinions about the principals' roles in instructional supervision.

The results reveal that over 40% of the teachers did not agree that principals were carrying out this role, even though the principals themselves have agreed that they were doing so. In addition, an average of the two scores would still find the principals falling below the acceptable level. As an instructional leader and supervisor, a principal should be managing instructional programmes that foster success for all students regardless of race, colour, or disability as posited by US Jefferson County Public Schools (2003). This translates to catering for the individual needs of students and must be embraced by all principals.

RESEARCH QUESTION 4:

Do principals monitor procedures on reporting students' progress to parents and stakeholders?

The mean score for this question of the teachers was 3.9, while the mean score for principals was 4.18. (See Table 3)

Table 3: Showing Frequency, Percent, Mean and S.D. for 'Reporting Students' Progress'

	Frequency		Percent		Mean Scores		Standard Deviations	
	Teacher	Principal.	Teacher	Principal	Teacher	Principal.	Teacher	Principal.
Valid 0	5	2	1.5	5.3	3.90	4.18	1.214	1.504
1	11	2	3.3	5.3				
2	34	2	10.2	5.3				
3	44	1	13.3	2.6				
4	106	5	31.9	13.2				
5	132	26	39.8	68.4				
Total	332	38	100.0	100.0				

The frequency reports again underscore the discrepancy in both respondents' scores as only 71.7% of teachers agreed that principals were carrying out this role. Conversely, 81.6% of the principals agreed that they were doing so. Drake and Roe (1999) underscored the importance of principals working together with teachers in formulating plans for evaluating and reporting students' progress. It is vital that parents and other stakeholders know of students' progress so that they can monitor and hold principals and teachers accountable for students' success.

RESEARCH QUESTION 5:

Do principals hold conferences prior to making classroom visits?

Table 4: Showing Frequency, Percent, Mean and S.D. for 'Holding-Pre-Conferences'

	Frequency		Percent		Mean Scores		Standard Deviations	
	Teacher	Principal.	Teacher	Principal	Teacher	Principal.	Teacher	Principal.
Valid 0	10	0	3.0	0	2.96	2.87	1.301	1.119
1	43	5	13.0	13.2				
2	61	10	18.4	26. 3				
3	91	9	27.4	23.7				
4	90	13	27.1	34.2				
5	37	1	11.1	2.6				
Total	332	38	100.0	100.0				

The mean scores from both respondents were significantly low. It was 2.96 on the teachers' questionnaire (TEPQ), and it corroborated almost perfectly with the mean score of 2.87 from the principals' questionnaire (PSEQ). This suggests that both groups of respondents did not agree that principals were carrying this role. So we can conclude that this particular task is not being done. If principals were not holding pre-conferences with teachers, this implies that classroom visits were not being used for its intended purpose-to improve instruction. One is inclined to wonder therefore, if classroom visits were used to catch teachers doing something wrong. The US National Association of Elementary Schools (2002) advised against this. Another implication could be that classroom visits were mainly used for summative evaluation. The education and training of principals are now held up to scrutiny, for if principals receive the adequate training in educational administration then pre-conferencing would feature strongly in their instructional role.

To further support the low scores, frequency reports in the table indicate that the percentages of teachers and principals who strongly agreed or agreed that principals were fulfilling this role are 38.2% and 36.8% respectively.

RESEARCH QUESTION 6:

Do principals visit classrooms regularly to observe teachers teach to ensure that students are meaningfully engaged in active learning?

Table 5: Showing Frequency, Percent, Mean and S.D. for 'Visit Classrooms Regularly'

		Frequency		Percent		Mean Scores		Standard Deviations	
		Teacher	Principal.	Teacher	Principal	Teacher	Principal.	Teacher	Principal.
Valid 0		5	0	1.5	0	3.43	4.00	1.233	.900
1		25	0	7.5	0				
2		40	4	12.0	10.5				
3		79	3	23.8	7.9				
4		117	20	35.2	52.6				
5		66	11	19.9	28.9				
Total		332	38	100.0	100.0				

Both respondent groups had mean scores of 3.43 and 4 respectively, which again indicate the disparity. (Table 1.5) The frequency results however, revealed that roughly 55.1 % of the teachers agreed or strongly agreed that principals were visiting classrooms regularly. Conversely, 81.5% principals agreed that they were carrying out these roles. The fact that 44.9% of the teachers did not agree or remained neutral is a cause for concern. Even when principals carry out classroom visits, the question that arises is why is it being done?

199

Glatthorn (1990), Calebrese and Zepeda (1997) as cited in Beach and Reinhartz (2000) and The US National Association of Elementary School Principals (2002) have all espoused the benefits of classroom observations which they said are useful for providing feedback, providing a baseline of data for assisting teachers, and for ensuring that students are actively involved in the teaching/learning process. However, Blase and Blase (2002) have posited that teachers seldom receive direct assistance in the form classroom observation (other than for formal evaluation). It is imperative therefore that principals undertake this role regularly and meaningfully.

RESEARCH QUESTION 7:

Do principals hold post conferences to provide feedback to teachers on strengths and weaknesses observed in classroom visits?

Table 6: Showing Frequency, Percent, Mean and S.D. for 'Post Conference'

	Frequency		Percent		Mean Scores		Standard Deviations	
	Teacher	Principal.	Teacher	Principal	Teacher	Principal.	Teacher	Principal.
Valid 0	5	0	1.5	0	3.70	4.24	1.248	.943
1	17	0	5.1	0				
2	36	4	10.8	10.5				
3	63	1	19.0	2.6				
4	105	15	31.6	39.5				
5	106	18	31.9	47.4				
Total	332	38	100.0	100.0				

As can be seen in table 1.6, the mean score of the teachers of 3.43 did not corroborate with the principals' mean score of 4.00, which suggests that the principals and teachers were not sharing similar views about the principals' function in post conferencing. This is further supported by the differences in the percentage of teachers (63.5%) and principals (86.9%) who strongly agreed or agreed that principals were facilitating post conferences.

No one can deny the benefits of post conferencing. It is critical to positive and purposeful classroom visits. It also forms the basis for feedback which taps into the basic human needs to improve, compete, and to be accurate and competent. The fact that 36.5% of teachers did not agree that principals were holding post conferences raises many questions.

RESEARCH QUESTION 8:

Do principals ensure that the major portion of contact time in school is spent on formal teaching/learning activities?

Table 7: Showing Frequency, Percent, Mean and S.D. for 'Contact Time'

	Frequency		Percent		Mean Scores		Standard Deviations	
	Teacher	Principal.	Teacher	Principal	Teacher	Principal.	Teacher	Principal.
Valid 0	1	0	.3	0	4.29	4.63	.863	.489
1	3	0	.9	0				
2	8	0	2.4	0				
3	37	0	11.1	0				
4	120	14	36.1	36.8				
5	163	24	49.1	63.2				
Total	332	38	100.0	100.0				

In response to research question 8, most teachers strongly agreed or agreed with a mean score of 4.29 and a percentage of 85.5. This again did not concur

201

favourably with the principals' mean score of 4.89 and percentage of 94.7. Even though the scores reflect the respondents' beliefs that principals were protecting the contact time, there is still some amount of disparity in the extent to which they agree. Loss of time can lead to loss of many resources as well as loss and lack of knowledge for the students who matter most in the overall scheme of education. In addition, Glatthorn (1990) has agreed that achievement is enhanced when time is maximised. It is critical therefore, that principals protect the contact time.

RESEARCH QUESTION 9:

Do principals coordinate the school's timetables to maximise use of instructional materials to promote learning objectives?

Table 8: Showing Frequency, Percent Mean and S.D. for 'Co-ordinate Time-Table'

	Frequency		Percent		Mean Scores		Standard Deviations	
	Teacher	Principal	Teacher	Principal	Teacher	Principal	Teacher	Principal
Valid 0	6	1	1.8	2.6	4.00	4.53	1.102	1.133
1	5	1	1.5	2.6				
2	15	1	4.5	2.6				
3	66	0	19.9	0				
4	105	6	31.6	15.8				
5	135	29	40.7	76.3				
Total	332	38	100.0	100.0				

The results for research question 9 showed noticeable difference in the mean scores of teachers and principals with scores of 4 and 4.53 respectively. Conversely, 72.3% of the teachers and 92.1% of principals held the opinion that principals co-ordinated the schools' timetables to maximise the use of teaching materials to promote learning. The differences in the principals and the teachers' responses were again evident. The standard deviations of 1.102 and 1.133 however, revealed little variance. On the whole the results revealed that respondent groups believed principals were basically carrying out this role.

RESEARCH QUESTION 10:

Do principals provide up-to-date teaching and learning materials for instruction?

Table 9: Showing Frequency, Percent Mean and S.D. for 'Up-to Date Teaching/Learning Materials'

	Frequency		Percent		Mean Scores		Standard Deviations	
	Teacher	Principal.	Teacher	Principal	Teacher	Principal.	Teacher	Principal.
Valid 0	3	0	.9	0	3.79	4.26	1.159	.724
1	9	0	5.7	0				
2	17	2	5.1	5.3				
3	69	0	20.8	0				
4	121	22	36.4	57.9				
5	103	14	31.0	36.8				
Total	332	38	100.0	100.0				

In response to research question 10, many teacher respondents were neutral with a mean score of 3.79 while the principals agreed that they carried out this role with a mean score of 4.26. The wide difference between the mean scores is indicative of the difference in the opinions of both groups of respondents. Frequency scores revealed that 72.3 % of teachers strongly agreed or agreed that principals were carrying out this role, while a resounding 94.7% of principals strongly agreed or agreed that they were carrying out the role. The fact that so many teachers agreed that principals were not providing up-to-date teaching / learning warrants serious attention. This is linked to the problem of limited resources which is a reality in the Jamaican education system. Nevertheless, teachers expect principals to provide them with the materials they need to perform their jobs well. In the US Jefferson County Public Schools' (2003), "Outstanding Administrative Profile", an outstanding administrator expects the use of technology in instruction. Hence if the administrator expects the use of technology, then it follows logically that he/she has to be committed to provide such technology.

Overall, each of the respondent groups agreed that principals were establishing criteria for academic standards, monitoring students progress, ensuring that the major portion of contact time was spent on formal teaching learning activities, and that principals were co-ordinating the school timetables to maximise the use of instructional materials for instruction. However, while the principals agreed that they were functional in carrying their role in instructional leadership with an overall average of 4.185, the teachers found them lacking on some counts with an overall average of 3.789.

In order to ascertain if there is any significant difference in the teachers and principals perceptions regarding the principals' roles in instructional leadership a paired sample t test was performed on the mean scores in this domain.

Table 10: Showing Paired Sample Statistics, Correlation and Test on the Mean Scores of Teachers and Principals Instructional Leadership

PAIRED SAMPLE STATISTICS

	Mean	n	Standard Deviation	Std. Mean Error
Pair 1 Teachers' Score	3.7890	10	.40421	.12782
Principals' Score	4.1850	10	.51887	.16408

PAIRED SAMPLE CORRELATIONS

	N	Correlation	Sig.
Pair 1 Teachers' & Principals' Scores	10	.933	.000

PAIRED SAMPLE TEST

		Paired Differences						
	Mean	Std. Deviation	Std Error Mean	95% Confidence Interval of the Difference				
				Lower	Upper	t	df	Sig.
Pair 1	-.3960	.20299	.06419	-.5412	-.2508	-6.169	9	.000

The results of the 'Paired Sample Statistics' confirmed the overall mean and provided the mean standard deviations for both sets of responses (table 4.16). The overall standard deviations revealed a significant variance of .20299 in the mean scores.

The 'Paired Sample Correlations' showed that there is a significant high positive correlation of .933 between the items with significance of .000. This means that to three decimal places $p<.001$. Hence there is a statistical significance where $p<0.05$. This underscores the difference between the two variables.

The 'Paired Sample Test' indicates a mean value of -.3960 which is the difference for the two variables in the paired sample statistics. Since the confidence interval does not contain zero, this indicates that the difference is significant. The associated significance reported as .000 means that to three decimal places p<.001 which underscores a statistical difference where p<0.05. The t value of –6.169 and a degree of freedom (df) of 9 yielded a t critical of 2.262 where p<0.05 (based on the Table of t values in Ary, Jacobs and Razavieh (1990)). Since the t value of –6.169 is less than the t critical of 2.262 we can reject any null hypothesis that there is no significant difference between the variables. This indicates that there is a significant difference in teachers and principals' perceptions regarding the principals' roles in instructional leadership.

These results further speak to the disparity in the perceptions of teachers and principals. The question that arises is-why is it that the principals and teachers are sharing opposing views re-the principals' involvement in instructional leadership? Is it that principals are trying their best, but that best is not good enough to meet the expectations of teachers? This is clearly linked to the different role expectations and role variables that Gordon and Schneider (1991) claimed are influencing principals' behaviour. According to them, among the various expectations, teachers expect principals to provide resources for teaching and learning, to build performance culture that broadens the way they function and assist them to attain the instructional skills and curricular materials necessary for them to teach effectively. This underpins the necessity for principals to garner all the available resources necessary to assist in carrying out the mandate for education.

CONCLUSION

The findings from the analyses revealed a general dissension between teachers' perceptions and those of principals. However, while Blase and Blase (1999), noted that it is normal for these perceptions to vary, the discrepancies should not be so frequent and obvious. The items merely asked the respondents to agree whether or not principals are carrying out certain instructional functions. This is based on their observation and as such should not be hard to do, because it is either the principals are doing so or not doing so.

The first four items dealt specifically with student performance. While the principals agreed that they carried out all the roles in this section, between 29-41% of the teachers did not agree that they promoted programmes for students' individual differences or monitored students' reports to parents and stakeholders. In the US Jefferson County Public Schools 'Outstanding Administrative Profile' (2003) a school leader manages instructional programmes for students regardless of race, colour or disability, hence principals in their capacity as instructional supervisors should promote programmes to meet students individual needs. Similarly, by not monitoring students' reports to parents and stakeholders, they are making themselves less accountable and credible.

The next group of questions (5-7) were connected with classroom observation. Question 5 sought information about the principals' involvement in pre-conferencing and both groups concurred on this by agreeing that this was not done. Based on this finding the researcher is inclined to conclude that this is a true reflection. Beach and Reinhartz (2000) have classified pre-conferencing as the most important stage of the clinical supervision cycle as it establishes the guidelines and procedures of what will follow. Moreover, as an element of instructional leadership, pre-conferencing provides an opportunity according to Davies (1991), of setting up conditions so as to significantly reduce the probabilities of error in both the acquisition and execution of human performance. Hence principals in their quest to empower teachers and improve students' performance must embrace this task wholeheartedly.

The teachers did not agree that principals visited classrooms regularly and held post conferences even though the principals agreed that they did so. These two tasks are linked to pre-conferencing and establish what will follow. Beach and Reinhartz (2000) and Gordon and Schneider (1991) have all underscored the importance of classroom visits as critical to teacher improvement and student achievement. Post conferences on the other hand provide the feedback that Checkley (2000) and Hill (1996) said, is necessary in redefining teaching and sets the stage for teacher growth and development.

While most teachers agreed that principals protected the contact time and coordinate timetable to ensure that the major part is spent on teaching/learning activities, nearly 25% of them did not agree also that principals provided up-to-date teaching learning materials. This speaks to one of the duties of an instructional leader as proposed by the Jefferson County Public School (US) Administrative Profile (2003). If a principal expects teachers to use up-to-date teaching/learning materials such as technology, it follows logically that they should provide such.

In general, 75% of the teachers basically agreed that principals were carrying out their roles in instructional leadership while 84% principals agreed that they carried out these roles. While 75% might seem an acceptable percentage, one has to take note of the 25% who did not agree. For this may be the difference between failure and success of many of our students. Instructional leadership eats at the heart of teaching and learning as it provides the direct contact and assistance given to teachers so that the instructional programme can meet the needs of the pupils it serves. Edmonds (1979) as cited in Griffith (1999) described an effective principal as involved in academic instruction by setting clear and high achievement goals, monitoring students' progress and is directly immersed in the day to day activities of the school. Concomitantly, Ash and Persall (1999) suggested that all rules, regulations, roles and work of the principal should be designed to support and enhance the staff's ability to design quality-learning experiences for all students.

REFERENCES

Ash, Ruth & Persall, Maurice (1999). The principal as chief learning officer. *National Association of Secondary School Principals,* 84 (66), 15-22.

Beach, Don M. & Reinhartz, Judy (2000). *Supervisory Leadership: Focus on Instruction,* Massachusetts: Allyn & Bacon.

Blasé, Joseph & Blasé, Jo, (1999). Principals' Instructional Leadership and Teacher Development: Teachers' Perspectives. *Educational Administration Quarterly,* 35(3) 349.

Blasé, Joseph & Blasé, Jo (2002). The Micropolitics of Instructional Supervision: A Call for Research. *Education Administration Quarterly* 38 (1) 6-44.

Checkley, K. (2000).The contemporary principal: new skills for a new age. *Education Update,* 43(3) 4-6, 8.

Davies, Ivor K. (1991). Instructional development as an art: one of the three faces of ID. Retrieved February 17, 2004 from http://216.109.117.135/search cache?p=instrctional+development&ei=UTF-8&cop=mss.

Directory Of Public Educational Institutions (2002). Kingston: Ministry of Education, Youth & Culture.

Drake, Thelbert L. & Roe, William H. (1999). *The Principalship* 5th Edition. New Jersey: Prentice Hall Inc.

The Education Regulation (1980). Ministry of Education: Kingston.

Glanz, J. (1995). Dilemmas of assistant principals in their supervisory role: reflections of an assistant principal. *Journal of School Leadership,* 4, 577-593.

Glatthorn, Allan A. (1990*). Supervisory Leadership- Introduction to Instructional Supervision.* London: Scott, Foresman/Little.

Gordon. Richard & Schneider, Gail T., (1991). *School Based leadership: Challenges and Opportunities.* Dabuque, IA: W.C. Brown.

Griffith, J. (1999). The School Leadership/School Climate Relation: Identification of School Configurations Associated with Change in Principals *Education Administration Quarterly* 35 (2) pp. 267-291.

Hill L. (1996). Building one to one work relationships. Retrieved November 11, 2003 from http://web.cba.neu.edu/ ~ewertheim/interper/feedback.htm.

Jefferson County Public Schools Administrative Employment Package (n.d.). Retrieved March 24, 2003 from http:// jeffcoweb.jeffco.k12.us/hr/admin/packet/profile.html.

Murphy, J. (1990). Principal instructional leadership in P. W. Thurston & L.S. Lotto (eds.), *Perspectives on School. Advances in Educational Administration* (Volume 1, Part B, 163-2000) Greenwich, CN: JAI Press Inc.

The National Association of Elementary School Principals (2002). Leading learning communities. Retrieved October 8, 2003 from http://naesp.org/clientfiles/Iicread.pdf.

Sergiovanni, T. J. & Starratt, R. J. (1998). *Supervision: A redefinition* (4th ed.), New York: McGraw-Hill.

St. Maurice, Henry (2002). Self –study of supervisory practices in beginning teacher terminations. *International Journal of Leadership in Education* 5 (1) 71-75.

Winter, P.A. & Dunaway, D.M. (1997). Reaction of teachers as Applicants to Principal Recruitment Practices in a Reform Environment: The Effects of Job Attributes, Job Satisfaction, Job Information Source and School Level. *Journal of Research Development In Education* 30 (3).

Youngs, P. & King, M. B. (2002). Principal leadership to build school capacity. *Educational Administrative Quarterly* 38 (5) 643-670.

Yusuf—Khalil, Yasmeen (2002). Checklist for Instructional Leaders. Paper prepared for New Horizon Activity for Primary Schools, Kingston: NHP.

Chapter 8

SECONDARY SCHOOL
PRINCIPALS' PERCEPTIONS OF
THE MANAGEMENT AND
CURRICULAR ROLES OF
LIBRARIANS IN JAMAICAN
SCHOOLS

MYRTLE ELAINE HARRIS

ABSTRACT

The research results reported here are from a larger study that looked at the perceptions of principals, teachers and librarians of the role of a school librarian. The research question was: What do principals perceive to be the role of a school librarian? The major finding was that there was stronger agreement about a librarian's traditional management and curricular support functions with progressively lower ratings for items that implied greater curricular involvement. Principals thought that providing leadership in the development of the school library programme was the most important function of a school librarian. Teaching students how to use library resources and equipment was viewed as a school librarian's primary curricular function. The implications of the survey findings for school library adminstration particularly in the context of principals' support for school librarians and school library programmes are discussed.

INTRODUCTION

The government, through its Ministry of Education, Youth and Culture, is the primary provider of education in Jamaica. Secondary education is offered in two cycles. The first cycle, targeting students of age 12 to 14, is offered from grade 7 to 9 in all types of secondary schools. This is the only cycle in schools classified as "all-age" and "primary and junior high". The second cycle lasts for two years (grades 10 and 11) and targets students 15 to 16 years old. This cycle is offered in secondary high, technical high and agricultural high schools. The category "secondary high" now includes schools that were termed "comprehensive high" at the time that the survey was conducted. Some schools offer two further years of education in grades 12 and 13.

The Ministry of Education and Youth has sought to address problems of access, quality and equity in secondary schools through the Reform of Secondary Education (ROSE). Achievements have included the introduction of a common curriculum for grades 7 to 9 and the provision of textbooks and other materials. The ROSE curriculum is student-centred and encourages activity-based learning, which should result in greater use of school libraries. Embedded in the curriculum is a range of information literacy skills (referred to as "learning skills"), some of which traditionally have been taught by librarians but will require collaboration with classroom teachers if they are to be taught effectively. These skills, which focus on areas such as the use and evaluation of information, prepare students for independent and lifelong learning in a global information environment that is complex and constantly changing.

School librarians are expected to provide curricular support. Some libraries receive technical and other support from the Jamaica Library Service through its Schools Library Network, which delivers services to schools on behalf of the Ministry of Education and Youth. There are six regional offices with direct responsibility for schools within each region. The regional offices maintain pool collections of materials in support of the curriculum. Among the other services provided are: bookmobile visits; technical support such as the acquisition and cataloguing of materials and advice on the planning and layout of school libraries; seminars and workshops for principals and teacher-librarians; and in-service training during scheduled visits to schools.

There are resource constraints in respect of staffing, funding, materials and equipment that impact on the quality of services delivered. The absence of national standards, policy guidelines and legislation for school libraries has resulted in a variation in the quality of resources and services provided. While standards for school libraries published by the Jamaica Library Association in 1971 were accepted by the Ministry of Education and Youth in principle, they have not been implemented because of the implications for funding (Mungo and Robertson, 1986). The result is that most libraries do not have adequate resources and many are without qualified librarians. Most have no computers with Internet access. Much will therefore depend on the commitment of the principal to the allocation of resources for the development of the school library.

There are no job descriptions that clearly outline the functions of school library staff although the requisite qualifications for an individual who may be classified as "librarian", "teacher-librarian" or "teacher with special responsibility for a school library" are outlined in *The Education Act: The Education Regulations, 1980 (1982)*. According to the Act, a librarian is "a person who has been awarded a degree or its equivalent from a university or other recognized institution that offers professional training in library studies" (such as the University of the West Indies). A teacher-librarian is "a person who holds a certificate or diploma of a trained teacher with an option in library science awarded by a teachers' college, college of education or other recognized institution that offers professional training for teachers" (such as The Mico College). A "teacher with special responsibility for a school library" is either (a) a trained teacher with a certificate or diploma with an option in library science awarded by a teachers college, college of education or other institution offering professional training for teachers, who assumes responsibility for a school library in addition to other teaching responsibilities or (b) a trained teacher who has successfully completed courses in school library routines. Implicit in the stated qualifications for the person with responsibility for a school library is the importance of training in both librarianship and teaching.

The functions of a school librarian as described by the Jamaica Library Association (1977, p. 2) include the selection of library materials, the organization and administration of the library and teaching the use of the library. Classroom teachers are expected to know what the library contains and how its resources can assist them in their teaching. The preparation of reading lists, displays of materials on various topics (including class projects), and suggestions for additions to the collection are some of the activities identified for co-operation and collaboration between classroom teachers and librarians. "The librarian should be...responsible to the principal of the school for the efficient administration of the library and for the planning and implementation of the school library programme" (Jamaica Library Association, 1977, p. 4)

Unfortunately, libraries and librarians have tended to be on the periphery of what takes place in schools. Noting the marginal role ascribed to libraries within the school system, Robinson (1991, p. 292) identifies some of the factors that account for the "negative concepts" held about school libraries. They include:

217

1. Inadequate provision for the proper maintenance of school libraries after they have been established.

2. School libraries that do not communicate the idea of "an active learning center at the hub of the educational programme"

3. The administering of the school library service by the public library system, which leads the school community to view the service as an "extension of the public library".

4. The practice of having unqualified personnel administering the school library with the result that the service is ineffective.

Nevertheless, libraries and librarians have the potential to make a valuable contribution to the attainment of educational goals and objectives; but the realization of this potential will to a large extent depend on the support of principals as administrators and instructional leaders. Principals' perceptions of the role of school libraries and librarians will impact on their level of support for libraries and ultimately the quality of the services that librarians can deliver. This chapter will first look at the role of school librarians and the perceptions held of their role as described in the literature. It will then show the results of a survey of the perceptions of secondary school principals in Jamaica and their implications for school library administration. The findings reported are from a larger study, which examined perceptions held of the role of a school librarian by principals, librarians and teachers in Jamaican public secondary schools. The term "school librarian" is used as the generic term to encompass other terms such as "teacher-librarian" and "media specialist" that are used in the literature for the professional with responsibility for the school library.

REVIEW OF THE RELEVANT LITERATURE

The researcher found in searching both the American and International ERIC databases that relevant citations were almost exclusively from the literature on school librarianship. The dearth of references noted is consistent with observations by Robinson (1991) and Hartzell (2002b). Indeed, what Robinson (1991, p. 291) describes as an "almost complete absence of any reference to school libraries" in the education literature of the Commonwealth Caribbean is, as she suggests, symptomatic of the marginal role ascribed to school libraries and librarians. This factor may help to explain the number of studies that have been done on perceptions held of the role of a school librarian.

The ideal role of school librarians as outlined in standards and other documents will be used as the starting point for a review of the research on perceptions held of the role of school librarians. *Information Power: Guidelines for School Library Media Programs* (American Association of School Librarians [AASL] & Association for Educational Communications and Technology [AECT], 1988) and *Information Power: Building Partnerships for Learning* (AASL & AECT, 1998), which form the point of reference for many of the perception studies that have been conducted, are illustrative. Although one study was found that looked at administrators' (principals, vice-principals and bursars) perceptions of school libraries, no Jamaican study that looked at principals' perceptions of school librarians was identified.

THE ROLE OF A SCHOOL LIBRARIAN

The role expectations of school librarians are outlined in standards, guidelines, and policy statements published by various government ministries with responsibility for education as well as professional bodies representing school librarians. (See, for example, Australia. New South Wales Department of Education and Training, 1987/2005; Canada. Alberta Education, 1984; Jamaica Library Association, 1971, 1977; AASL & AECT, 1988, 1998; International Association of School Librarianship, 1993; IFLA/ UNESCO, 2002). It should be noted that the publications of the Jamaica Library Association (now the Library and Information Association of Jamaica) are long overdue for revision so that they can better reflect library trends in the 21st century.

Information Power: Guidelines for School Library Media Programs (AASL& AECT, 1988) describes three "separate but overlapping roles" – information specialist, teacher and instructional consultant – through which the school librarian links the resources and services of the school library to the information needs and interests of staff and students. Through these roles the school librarian provides:

- access to information and ideas by assisting students and staff in identifying information resources and in interpreting and communicating intellectual content;
- formal and informal instruction in information skills, the production of materials, and the use of information and instructional technologies; and
- recommendations for instructional planning to individual teachers as well as assistance in schoolwide planning of curricular and instructional activities.

It is noted that, while the librarian frequently performs these roles "in concert with each other", the degree of emphasis on any one role may vary from school to school depending on the goals, priorities and resources of each school.

In the later publication, *Information Power: Building Partnerships for Learning* (1998), four related roles – teacher, instructional partner, information specialist and programme administrator – are described. The role of instructional "partner" replaces that of instructional "consultant" suggesting a shift in the librarian's role relationship with the teacher. The administrative functions of the librarian are also recognized in the additional role of "program administrator" described. This publication includes information literacy standards for student learning as well as guidelines for school librarians in the three major areas of their work identified: learning and teaching, information access and programme administration. It promotes collaboration, leadership and technology as important aspects of the school library programme.

PRINCIPALS' PERCEPTIONS OF A
SCHOOL LIBRARIAN'S ROLE

Shifts in role expectations described in successive standards for school librarians have been the result of changes in educational philosophy evident in the movement from a teacher-centred to a more learner-centred paradigm (Mohajerin and Smith, 1981; Stripling, 1996; O'Neal, 2004). With these changes, the role of the school librarian has evolved from that of "keeper of books" with a focus on administrative tasks and the organization of materials in support of teacher-directed learning to that of teacher and instructional partner collaborating with teachers to facilitate student-centred learning. However, the literature shows a time lag between the practised instructional role and that described in the literature. (Craver, 1984; Pickard, 1993). Indeed, in reviewing the literature, Mohajerin and Smith (1981) found that this "emerging role" of the school librarian represented the opinion of leaders in the field (that is, library/media educators and leaders of state and national professional associations and advisory agencies). They correctly point out that "to achieve maximum effectiveness in the school program ...the changed role ...must also be recognized and understood by teachers and principals" (Mohajerin and Smith, 1981, p. 152).

Studies have shown that principals place greater emphasis on librarians' administrative and information specialist functions than on their curricular role. For example, in a study by Edwards (1989) in Arizona, principals rated instruction seventh in importance of ten skills identified, while Reference/Resource to Students and Reference/Resource to Teachers – more traditional information service functions – were rated third and fifth in importance respectively. Similarly, Materials Selection, Library Management, and Reading Promotion - all traditional functions - were rated first, second and fourth, while Curriculum Planning and Audiovisual Production were rated ninth and tenth respectively.

Dorrell and Lawson (1995) in research done in Missouri also found that principals rated traditional library functions as the most important. Respondents gave the highest rating of importance to materials selection, library management, and reference services to students. Dorrell and Lawson found that tasks such as conferences with teachers and curriculum planning, which clearly indicated an "involvement within the instructional process of the school", were rated as being only of average importance. While principals believed that librarians should have some classroom teaching experience, they agreed that it was not necessary for them to be directly involved in curriculum planning and development. Dorrell and Lawson concluded that there was a discrepancy between the principals' perceptions of the role of the school librarian and what was advocated in *Information Power*.

In a survey conducted in 17 traditional high schools in Kingston, St. Andrew and St. Catherine, Jamaica, James (1999) looked at administrators' (principals, vice-principals and bursars) perceptions of school libraries. Although there should be caution in the use of the findings since only 35% of the respondents were principals, they may be used as indicators of their perceptions. James found that responses were focused on the school library's traditional functions as a centre for storing, organizing and circulating materials in support of the curriculum. Most respondents (75%) strongly agreed that the teacher-librarian should teach information skills and meet with teaching teams or individual teachers to identify their needs for instructional materials. However, only 5% strongly agreed that the teacher-librarian should plan lessons cooperatively with teachers, and only 7.5% strongly agreed that he/she should be a member of the curriculum planning team. With respect to preparing the budget for the school library programme, 80% of the respondents disagreed, while only 45% agreed that the school librarian is responsible for establishing polices for the operation of the school library. James's findings suggest that administrators placed stronger emphasis on curriculum support than on the management or curricular functions of school librarians.

Hauck (1985) surveyed the perceptions of principals and teacher-librarians in 177 schools in

Alberta. The focus of the research by Hauck was the perceptions of teacher-librarians and principals of what the role of the teacher-librarian was then and should be in the future. The research followed publication of the document, *Policy, Guidelines, Procedures and Standards for School Libraries in Alberta* (Canada, Alberta Education, 1984), which placed emphasis on the integration of the school library programme into the total curriculum, and the leadership role required of the principal in achieving this. Hauck found that, at that time, teacher-librarians saw their role in curriculum and instruction as the most important, while principals rated this role as being fourth in importance. Where consensus existed between the two groups then, the traditional role of manager seemed to be regarded as important, with the provision of information services and selection of materials in second and third places respectively. Many of the functions considered to be important at that time by teacher-librarians, but not by principals, related to involvement in curriculum and instruction. On the other hand, most of the tasks considered important by principals but not teacher-librarians were traditional "librarian" tasks (for example, "Inform teachers regularly about new learning resources and technology"). However, Hauck found that there was much greater consensus between the teacher-librarians and principals surveyed about desirable roles for the teacher-librarian in the future. This was evident in greater agreement on role statements relating to curriculum and instruction. Both groups also had greater agreement on the importance of several organization and management role statements.

The literature suggests that there is strongest emphasis on the librarian's role as information specialist providing support for the curriculum. There is some support for the librarian's management role but least agreement about the curricular role.

RESEARCH DESIGN AND METHODOLOGY

The purpose of the study was to determine perceptions held of the role of a school librarian. A descriptive survey research design was used. The population comprised principals, librarians and teachers of five core subjects in each of 141 Jamaican public secondary schools with libraries – 58 secondary high, 70 comprehensive high and 13 technical high schools. A stratified random sample was drawn from these three types of schools including 24 comprehensive high (50%), 19 secondary high (40%) and 5 technical high (10%). The responses of principals from these 48 schools are the focus of this chapter. The research question was: What do principals perceive to be the role of a school librarian?

A three-part questionnaire was administered to principals. Part I was concerned with demographic data relating to the age, gender, education and training of participants and subjects taught, if any. Part II sought to determine the extent to which participants agreed with statements pertaining to the functions of a school librarian. Derived from school library standards and the literature on school librarianship, the statements were related to six major areas of professional activity: management, curriculum, resource provision, services to students, services to teachers and advocacy. The following three areas are the focus of this chapter (See Appendix):

a) **Management** (For example leadership, planning, training staff, and writing annual reports)

b) **Curriculum** (For example, direct teaching or cooperation and collaboration with teachers in the delivery of the curriculum)

c) **Resources** (For example, selection, acquisition and organization of resources)

A five-point Likert-type scale was used to measure the perceptions of participants. Five (5) was the highest point on the scale, indicating functions that a school librarian "definitely should" perform. One was the lowest point, indicating functions that a school librarian "definitely should not" perform.

Part III of the questionnaire elicited data on those functions of a school librarian that participants ranked as the five most important functions of a school librarian. In this section, "1" indicated the function ranked as most important. Respondents were given an opportunity to add any other comments on the functions of a school librarian in response to the only open-ended question.

Data were collected between December 1999 and January 2000. Thirty-eight questionnaires (79.2%) were returned including 20 comprehensive high schools (83.3%), 16 secondary high (84.2%) and 2 technical high (40%).

RESEARCH FINDINGS

PRINCIPALS' PERCEPTIONS

MANAGEMENT

The school librarian is responsible for planning and managing the school library (IFLA/UNESCO, 2002) and is responsible to the principal for its efficient administration (Jamaica Library Association, 1977). The principal's perception of the librarian's management role will influence how administrative decisions are made about the school library. Table 1 shows principals' perceptions of a school librarians' management role.

An overwhelming majority of the principals (94.70%) thought that librarians definitely should provide leadership in the development of the school library programme. Responses to this item had a very high mean (M = 4.95) and little variation (SD = 0.23) showing very strong agreement among principals about the importance of school librarians' leadership role in the development of the school library programme.

Table 1: Principals' Perceptions of School Librarian's Management Role (no. and %)

Role	Def Sh	Sh	Und	Sh not	Def Sh Not	Total	M	SD
Provide leadership	36 94.70	2 5.30	0	0	0	38	4.95	0.23
Establish procedures	32 86.50	4 10.80	1 2.70	0	0	37	4.84	0.44
Advise the principal	29 76.30	9 23.70	0	0	0	38	4.76	0.43
Train persons	16 43.20	18 48.60	3 8.10	0	0	37	4.35	0.63
Write annual reports	26 70.30	10 27.00	1 2.70	0	0	37	4.68	0.53
Plan for the efficient use of space, facilities, and equipment	30 78.90	8 21.10	0	0	0	38	4.79	0.41
Prepare the budget	23 62.20	14 37.80	0	0	0	37	4.62	0.49

Note. Def = definitely; Sh = should; Und = undecided

A large majority of the respondents thought that school librarians definitely should establish procedures for the operation of the school library (86.50%); plan for the efficient use of space, facilities, and equipment in the school library (78.90%); and advise the principal on appropriate library furniture and equipment (76.30%). Mean scores for these items were high and respondents' answers did not show much variation (M = 4.84, SD = 0.44; M = 4.79, SD = 0.41; and M = 4.76, SD = 0.43 respectively). A majority also thought that a school librarian definitely should write annual reports on the school library (70.30%) and prepare the budget for the school library (62.20%). There was least agreement in respect of training persons who work in the school library (M = 4.35, SD = 0.63). Some respondents may have been of the view that training is the responsibility of the Jamaica Library Service.

CURRICULUM

The literature emphasizes the importance of the librarian's teaching role. Collaboration with teachers to teach information literacy skills is expected. Principals' perceptions of a school librarian's curricular role are presented in Table 3.

Table 2: Principals' Perceptions of School Librarian's Curricular Role (no. and %)

Role	Def Sh	Sh	Und	Sh not	Def Sh not	Total	M	SD
Familiarize self with curriculum guides	30 78.90	8 21.10	0	0	0	38	4.79	0.41
Teach students	34 91.90	3 8.10	0	0	0	37	4.92	0.28
Collaborate with subject teachers	24 64.90	13 35.10	0	0	0	37	4.65	0.48
Stimulate students' interest in literature	17 45.90	17 45.90	3 8.10	0	0	37	4.38	0.64
Encourage critical and independent use of resources	23 60.50	15 39.50	0	0	0	38	4.61	0.50
Team teach units	16 43.20	19 51.40	2 5.40	0	0	37	4.38	0.59
Participate in the evaluation of units	9 23.70	19 50.00	10 26.30	0	0	38	3.97	0.72
Develop programme independently	13 34.20	10 26.30	8 21.10	4 10.50	3 7.90	38	3.68	1.28
Teach students to use computers	10 27.00	20 54.10	5 13.50	2 5.40	0	37	4.03	0.80
Participate in meetings of subject departments	2 5.30	27 71.10	7 18.40	1 2.60	1 2.60	38	3.74	0.72
Work with teachers to integrate resources	17 44.70	19 50.00	2 5.30	0	0	38	4.40	0.60

Note. Def = definitely; Sh = should; Und = undecided

An overwhelming majority of the principals (91.90%) agreed that a school librarian definitely should perform the traditional role of teaching students how to use library resources and equipment. This item had a high mean score and showed little variation in respondents answers (M = 4.92, SD = 0.28). A majority of the respondents also thought that a school librarian definitely should familiarize him/herself with curriculum guides and textbooks (78.90%); collaborate with subject teachers in developing students' research and study skills (64.90%); and encourage students in the critical and independent use of library resources (60.50%).

Ratings were progressively lower for items that implied greater curricular involvement. Thus, only 43.20% of the respondents agreed that a school librarian definitely should team teach units requiring the use of library resources. An even lower percentage of the respondents thought that a school librarian definitely should participate in the evaluation of units taught collaboratively (23.70%) and participate in meetings of subject departments (5.30%). However, although there were progressively lower ratings for items that implied greater curricular involvement, a majority of them were positive – team teach units (94.60%); participate in the evaluation of units taught collaboratively (73.70%) and participate in the meetings of subject departments (76.40%). Similarly, only 27% thought that school librarians definitely should teach students how to use computers, but a large majority (81.10%) agreed that they should. This suggests some degree of support for the librarian's curricular role.

Developing a programme of library and information skills for students independently of subject teachers was the item about which there was least agreement

(M = 3.68, SD = 1.28) among respondents. A total of 18.40% thought that a school librarian either should not or definitely should not develop a programme independently, while 21% of them were undecided. There is strong support in the literature for the view that these skills should not be taught independently in the library.

RESOURCE PROVISION

Providing resources in support of the curriculum is a core function of school librarians. Table 2 shows principals' perceptions of a school librarian's role in relation to resource provision.

A large majority of the principals thought that librarians definitely should select resources (81.60%); organize resources (86.50%); and ensure that resources were up-to-date (81.10%). Their responses were very positive and showed little variation (M = 4.82, SD = 0.39; M = 4.87, SD = 0.35; and M = 4.81, SD = 0.40 respectively), suggesting strong agreement about a school librarian's role in providing resources.

Table 3: Principals' Perceptions of School Librarian's Role in Relation to Resource Provision (no. and %)

Role	Def Sh	Sh	Und	Sh not	Def sh not	Total	M	SD
Select resources	31 81.60	7 18.40	0	0	0	38	4.82	0.39
Organize resources	32 86.50	5 13.50	0	0	0	37	4.87	0.35
Ensure resources are up-to-date	30 81.10	7 18.90	0	0	0	37	4.81	0.40
Acquire resources from other institutions	11 29.70	25 67.60	1 2.70	0	0	37	4.27	0.51

Note. Def = definitely; Sh = should; Und = undecided

PRINCIPALS' RANKING OF MOST IMPORTANT FUNCTIONS

Principals ranked providing leadership in the development of the school library programme as the most important function of a school librarian. They ranked as the five most important functions in descending order:

- Provide leadership in the development of the school library programme
- Organize resources in the school library through a system of cataloguing, classification and indexing
- Teach students how to use library resources and equipment
- Establish procedures for the operation of the school library
- Select resources for the school library

It is interesting to note that only the traditional curricular function – teaching students how to use library resources and equipment – is included. All other functions pertain to management and resource provision. Their ranking reinforced their agreement about the primacy of the librarian's roles as manager and provider of curricular support.

RESPONSES TO OPEN-ENDED QUESTION

Principals were given the opportunity to express their views in response to an open-ended question, which solicited "any other comments concerning the functions of a school librarian". Their responses were:

"Librarian should try to create a welcoming atmosphere in the Library.

He or she should maintain discipline without alienating the students.

He or she should make the Library attractive and interesting even just to look at" (Principal, Secondary High School)

"1. Audit the library resources/materials annually and prepare inventory for principal.

2. Ensure that the atmosphere in the library is conducive to learning and research at all times." (Principal, Comprehensive High School)

"Provide opportunities for students to read for Leisure." (Principal, Comprehensive High School)

"Encourage students, teachers and community to add to library resources." (Principal, Technical High School)

"The aim of the school is to get the library equipped and to function as a learning centre" (Principal, Comprehensive High School)

In summary, responses were focused on the librarian's management and support roles in providing and accounting for resources; encouraging recreational reading; and creating an environment in the library that is welcoming and conducive to study. There was no reference to the librarian's role as teacher or curriculum partner.

CONCLUSIONS AND IMPLICATIONS

The survey results show that, overall, principals' perceptions of the school librarian's management and curricular roles were positive. However, there was stronger agreement about the librarian's traditional management and resource support functions and progressively lower ratings for items that implied greater curricular involvement. These are indicators that principals perceived the librarian as the provider of resources in support of teaching and learning rather than as a partner in the delivery of the curriculum as promoted in library standards and guidelines. Their stronger emphasis on the librarian's traditional management and curricular support roles is consistent with the findings of Hauck (1985), Edwards (1989) and Dorrell and Lawson (1995). While there is also support for the findings of

James (1999) in respect of their emphasis on curricular support, the survey findings differ concerning their perceptions of a school librarian's management role.

Providing leadership in the development of the school library programme was perceived to be the most important function of a school librarian. However, in developing and implementing a programme successfully, the support of the principal will be critical. There is strong consensus in the literature that the support of principals as administrators and instructional leaders is essential if school librarians are to perform their functions effectively. For example, the librarian needs support for developing the information skills curriculum and integrating the school library programme (Haycock, 1998; O'Neal, 2004). Principals' expectations and support for team planning with teachers will impact on librarians' level of involvement in that activity (Tallman, 1995); and they will need to provide opportunities for librarians and teachers to plan together formally, beginning with appropriate scheduling arrangements (Lewis, 1991). In addition, factors that help to determine the quality of school library programmes such as the size and the currency of the library collection and the presence of a qualified librarian are in some way under the principal's influence, if not direct control (Hartzell, 2002a). Thus, librarians' effectiveness in the management and curricular roles that principals perceived that they should be performing is to some extent dependent on their active support.

Teaching students how to use library resources and equipment was perceived to be a school librarian's primary teaching function. This is probably due to a lack of understanding or appreciation of the potential of school librarians to contribute to curricular goals and objectives. Nevertheless, principals agreed that librarians should collaborate with subject teachers in developing students' research and study skills. Conversely, there was some disagreement about developing a programme of library and information skills independently in the library – a view that is supported by the literature. It is important for school librarians to be equipped with the requisite qualifications in both education and librarianship if they are to be expected to collaborate with teachers to team teach units requiring the use of library resources or participate in the evaluation of units taught collaboratively with teachers.

Although technical support is available from the Jamaica Library Service, persons with responsibility for school libraries will need to have knowledge and skills in the field of school librarianship to successfully perform their professional functions.

Establishing procedures for the operation of the school library (ranked fourth in importance) is a function that should be performed by a librarian with the professional training to do so efficiently and effectively. Similarly, a qualified librarian is better equipped to make decisions about the selection and organization of resources and the delivery of services in support of the curriculum.

Principals who support school librarians and school library programmes have positive perceptions about their contributions to teaching and learning (Oberg, 2006). It is evident that respondents did not perceive these contributions to include active involvement in curricular activities. This view is contrary to that promoted within the school library profession. There is need for a national policy as well as standards and guidelines for the development of school libraries – an issue discussed at a National Forum on School Libraries held in Jamaica in 2006. Their successful development and implementation should assist efforts to develop and implement effective school library programmes.

Of particular importance is the preparation of principals and school librarians. Writing in the context of the United States, Gary Hartzell, a professor of educational administration and a former principal, notes that although principals know that librarians teach research skills, "they usually do not perceive them as teachers in the same sense as their colleagues in the classroom" (Hartzell, 2002b, p. 93). Contending that too few principals understand the value of the school library and the school librarian, he attributes this to factors such as the absence of information on issues pertaining to school libraries and the role of school librarians in either the journals or the conference programmes of interest to administrators. Pointing to "the tendency of administrative preparation programmes to focus on potential problems rather than on demonstrated or possible benefits" of school library programmes, Hartzell (2002b, p. 103) further observes that "without exposure to the merits of library media programs during their training, principals in the field generally have neither the inclination nor the time to learn about them on their own". The writer supports this view and recommends that Jamaican principals be exposed to information on school libraries and the role of school librarians both through formal and informal training. A course in the professional preparation programme of school principals that focuses on the role of the school library and librarian is a predictor for higher ratings of their importance (Alexander, 2003). With respect to school librarians, formal or informal training in advocacy is of particular importance in equipping them to effectively communicate to the school community the role of school libraries and librarians in the attainment of educational goals and objectives.

Consideration should also be given to greater collaboration between institutions or departments responsible for training principals and librarians in order to address any gaps in programme content. Improvements in the preparation of both principals and librarians will help to ensure that libraries and librarians play a meaningful role in Jamaican schools.

Much research has been done internationally on perceptions held of the role of school librarians and on principal support. The literature on education and school librarianship in the Caribbean would benefit from further research on principals' perceptions and other factors that impact on their support for school librarians and school library programmes.

BIBLIOGRAPHY

Alexander, Linda B. (2003). Education reform and the school library media specialist: Perceptions of principals. *Knowledge Quest, 32* (2), 10-13.

American Association of School Librarians (AASL) & Association for Educational Communications and Technology (AECT). (1988). *Information power: Guidelines for school library media programs.* Chicago: American Library Association; Washington, DC: AECT.

American Association of School Librarians (AASL) & Association for Educational Communications and Technology (AECT). (1998). *Information power: Building partnerships for learning.* Chicago: American Library Association.

Australia. New South Wales Department of Education and Training (2005). Library Policy – Schools. Retrieved February 15, 2007 from the Department's Web site at: https://www.det.nsw.edu.au/policies/curriculum/schools/libraries/ PD20050221.shtml. (Original document published 1987)

Canada, Alberta Education. (1984). *Policy, guidelines, procedures and standards for school libraries in Alberta.* N. p.: Alberta Education.

Craver, Kathleen W. (1986). The changing instructional role of the library media specialist: 1950-84: A survey of professional literature, standards, and research studies. *School Library Media Quarterly, 14* (4), 183-191.

Dorrell, Larry D. & Lawson, V. Lonnie. (1995). What are principal's perceptions of the school library media specialist? *NASSP Bulletin, 79* (573), 72-80.

The Education Act: The Education Regulations, 1980 (1982). Kingston, Jamaica: The Government Printer.

Edwards, Karlene K. (1989). Principals' perceptions of librarians: A survey. *School Library Journal, 35* (5), 28-31.

Harris, Myrtle Elaine (2003). *Perceptions of Jamaican secondary school principals,* teachers and librarians of the role of librarians in secondary schools. Unpublished master's thesis, University of the West Indies, Mona.

Hartzell, Gary (2002a). The multiple dimensions of principal involvement. *School Libraries Worldwide 8* (1), 43-48.

Hartzell, Gary (2002b). The principal's perceptions of school libraries and teacher-librarians. *School Libraries Worldwide 8* (1), 92-110.

Hauck, Philomena (1985). The role of the teacher-librarian in Alberta schools. *School Libraries in Canada, 5* (4) 18-26.

Haycock, Ken (1998). Leadership by secondary school principals. *Teacher Librarian, 26* (2), 32.

The IFLA/UNESCO school library guidelines. (2002). Retrieved December 2002 from IFLA's Web site at: http:// www.ifla.org/VII/s11/pubs/sguide02.pdf

International Association of School Librarianship (IASL). (1993). Policy statement on school libraries. Seattle: IASL.

Jamaica Library Association. (1971). *School library standards.* Kingston: The Association.

Jamaica Library Association. (1977). *Suggestions for teacher-librarians.* Kingston: The Association.

James, Janet. (1999). *School administrators' perception of school libraries: A survey of select secondary schools.* Unpublished MLS research paper, University of the West Indies, Mona.

Lewis, Carol Gaskins. (1991). The role of the library media program in the middle school. *School Library Media Annual, 9,* 129-41.

Mohajerin, Kathryn S. & Smith, Earl P. (1981). Perceptions of the role of the school media specialist. *School Media Quarterly, 9* (3), 152-63.

Mungo, Katie M. and Amy Robertson, comps. (1986). *Policy Guidelines for School Library Development.* [Kingston]: Jamaica Library Association and Commonwealth Library Association.

Oberg, Dianne (2006). Developing the respect and support of school administrators. *Teacher Librarian, 33* (3), 13-18.

O'Neal, Anita J. (2004). Administrators', teachers', and media specialists' perceptions of the roles of media specialists in the schools' instructional programs: implications for instructional administration.

Pickard, Patricia W. (1993). The instructional consultant role of the school library media specialist. *School Library Media Quarterly, 21* (2), 115-121.

Robinson, Cherrell V. (1991). The School library: A valuable partner in the search for educational excellence. In *Proceedings of the 1990 Cross-Campus Conference on Education* (pp. 291-296). Kingston: The University of the West Indies, Faculty of Education.

Stripling, Barbara K (1996). Quality in school library programs: Focus on learning. *Library Trends, 44* (3), 631-56.

Tallman, Julie I. (1995). Curriculum consultation: Strengthening activity through multiple-content area units. *School Library Media Quarterly, 24* (1), 27-34.

APPENDIX: MAJOR AREAS OF PROFESSIONAL ACTIVITY

A. MANAGEMENT

A school librarian should:

- provide leadership in the development of the school library programme.
- establish procedures for the operation of the school library.
- advise the principal on appropriate library furniture and equipment.
- train persons who work in the school library.
- write annual reports on the school library.
- plan for the efficient use of space, facilities, and equipment in the school library.
- prepare the budget for the school library.

B. CURRICULUM

A school librarian should:

- familiarize him/herself with curriculum guides and textbooks.
- teach students how to use library resources and equipment.
- collaborate with subject teachers in developing students research and study skills.
- develop programmes to stimulate students' interest in and appreciation for literature.
- encourage students in the critical and independent use of library resources.
- collaborate with teachers to team teach units requiring the use of library resources.
- participate in the evaluation of units taught collaboratively with teachers.
- develop a programme of library and information skills for students independently of subject teachers.
- teach students how to use computers for access to information.
- participate in meetings of subject departments.
- work cooperatively with teachers to integrate library resources with classroom programmes and activities.

C. RESOURCES

A school librarian should:

- select resources for the school library.
- organize resources in the school library through a system of cataloguing, classification, and indexing.

- take steps to ensure that the library's resources are up-to-date.
- acquire information and resources from other institutions for staff and students.

MYRTLE ELAINE HARRIS

Chapter 9

TEACHERS' AND STUDENTS' PERCEPTIONS OF VOCATIONAL AND TECHNICAL EDUCATION PROGRAMME PLANNING IN JAMAICAN HIGH SCHOOLS

EARL CHRISTIAN &
AUSTIN EZENNE

ABSTRACT

Although there is a planning unit in the Ministry of Education Youth and Culture in Jamaica, there are still many problems associated with the planning of Vocational and Technical Education Programmes. Vocational and Technical Education subjects are still being rated as inferior compared to Traditional subjects, and there is public outcry for a more competent workforce. At the same time, less time is spent in the Vocational and Technical Education courses in the schools. Not many "A" students opt to undertake studies in this type of education. The purpose of this study was to investigate the perceptions of teachers and students about the planning of Vocational and Technical Education Programmes in selected High schools, in Jamaica.

The complex nature of Vocational and Technical Education together and the need for human and material resources, make it necessary for careful planning of the programme. On the other hand, the general low performance of many students in their final examinations has made it necessary to investigate the perceptions about the curriculum, the quality and quantity of teachers as well as students' performance, and other internal factors, which all have implications for the planning of Vocational and Technical Education Programmes, for the nation.

A convenient sample of 58 High School teachers of Vocational and Technical Education subjects as well as 316 Grade 11 students was chosen. In order to collect the data, Questionnaires were administered to students and teachers, and analyzed by using frequencies and percentages.

The findings suggest that not only did teachers need greater opportunity to participate in the planning process of Vocational and Technical Education Programmes, but they also needed more resource materials, more hands-on approach, reduced class sizes, and adequate budgetary allocations. Students needed to be more involved in planning, and to know that on completion their skills are needed at the workplace.

INTRODUCTION AND BACKGROUND

Vocational and Technical Education is a most valuable body of knowledge and series of activities that provide individuals with aptitudes and skills, which will not only lead to personal development but will also help individuals to respond positively to the changing demands of a dynamic economy and a more efficient workforce. Vocational and Technical Education is the connecting link between the school system and the employment market. (Bastick and Ezenne, 2003)

The Ministry of Education Youth and Culture has adopted a holistic approach to the provision of education, and the caliber of the secondary level graduates which has involved the entire educational system. The programmes offered at the secondary level include Agriculture, Home Economics, Business Education, Visual Arts, Construction, Commercial and Industrial Education and funded by the Government of Jamaica and the World Bank under the Reform of Secondary Education (ROSE) project. This approach is designed to accomplish widespread reform at all post primary levels, and incorporates a common curriculum, which includes Resource and Technology (R&T) as pre-vocational courses at the Grades 7-9 levels. (Education Sector Survey, 1973)

Given the complex nature of Vocational and Technical education, careful planning is extremely necessary in order to ensure proper implementation and greater efficiency. Planning considerations include planning for curriculum development, staff development, policymaking, planning for decision-making, instructional improvement, physical, material, time, as well as human and financial resources.

Government's new policy to promote equity, access and quality at the Post Primary level has also made it necessary to approach planning in a more comprehensive and collaborative manner, bringing together pertinent stakeholders, including teachers and students in the planning and implementation process of Vocational and Technical programmes in the schools. New curricula have been developed, additional facilities provided, teachers trained and the introduction of Vocational and Technical subjects by HEART/NTA (White Paper, 2001).

The perceptions of teachers and students of the planning of Vocational and Technical Education Programmes will therefore greatly impact on the level of commitment, motivation and innovativeness on the part of the teachers as well as the level of performance of the students, which have the potential to influence the teaching and learning processes within the school. It will also provide well-needed feedback, which will inform measures to be taken to enhance the programmes. The teachers are expected to ensure that quality instruction is available to students, and the students on the other hand stand to benefit optimally if proper planning is practiced.

Institutional planning should be directed not only to ensure maximum efficiency and flexibility in the use of resources, but also foster collaboration with specialist teachers, with due regards for prevailing local factors and relevant research. Adequate funds should be allocated for recurrent expenditure for supplies and maintenance and repair of equipment.

Intricately connected to the planning process of Vocational and Technical Education Programmes is the need to ensure not only greater participation in this non-traditional form of education but also to ensure improved performance in the terminal examination at the high school level. The marginal connotations and the debilitating perceptions will however have to be addressed. According to a former Minister of Education, Phyllis Mitchell (1999), the dictates of modern society are steeped in technology, and mandate the preparation of a workforce, which is adequately equipped to withstand the rigors of global competition.

The need for careful planning is also driven by the prevailing shortcomings, which according to Mitchell, (1999), are: inadequate supplies of equipment and tools, sub-optimal infrastructure arrangements, shortage of qualified instructors/teachers, and poor alignment with market needs.

Inherent in the planning process is the need for information – what skills are needed in society, what jobs offer the best opportunities to individuals at present and in the future, what employment sectors are developing and require skilled manpower. The educational system should be adjusted to meet changing needs and backed up by some means of evaluating policy objectives and planning, which are inseparable (UNESCO Report, 1984).

THEORETICAL FRAMEWORK

In order for goals and objective to be achieved it is of extreme importance that careful planning be undertaken. This may entail the utilization of all available resources, human resource being the dominant feature. According to Musaazi (1982), planning is a rational process of preparing a set of decisions for future actions directed at achieving goals and objectives by optimal means. The planning process of Vocational and Technical Education, like in any other field, has a significant impact on the level of success experienced, as pointed out in a UNESCO report (1984).

The document supports the view that the development and expansion of Vocational and Technical Education are for the most part an integral element in national development planning and so in most countries there is a planning department in the administrative structure of the Educational System

One of the problems and perhaps the major one inhibiting sound planning is the lack of information such as: required standards of competences for certain jobs, relevance of certain skills, prior knowledge of the number of students to be catered for in a course, the costs involved, students' assessment, available material resources, requirements of immediate employers and the future potentials and direction of a given vocation. If realistic planning is to take place, there should be adequate information on all of the above and more.

The Vocational and Technical Unit of the Ministry plays a vital role in promoting Vocational and Technical Education, in that in addition to fostering the development of potential for self-expression, creativity and inventiveness, it also assumes a major role in the development and implementation of teacher programmes that will produce the caliber of teachers who are qualified to contribute to the achievement of foregoing goals.

According to Calhoun and Finch (1982): "Providing an adequate curriculum is the most important function of the school system". He concluded that, "The curriculum is affected by administrative policies of the school, teacher competence, philosophy of the school, school equipment and facilities, findings of educational research, instructional materials, school personnel policies, parent-teacher relationships, community culture and environment, socio-economic trend and support from the state.

Historically, technical and vocational education have never been preferred above traditional grammar school or academic disciplines. In fact it has always been regarded as inferior education, and to support this notion many students who displayed high performance were sent to traditional high schools, while those who were considered not so brilliant would be offered places in Technical, Secondary and Comprehensive High Schools, now reclassified as high schools.

The reclassification of Secondary Education under the government's new Reform of Secondary Education (ROSE) policy seeks to promote equity, access and quality at the post primary level, in order to minimize the diversity. This new thrust has made it necessary to approach planning in a more comprehensive and collaborative manner, bringing together pertinent stakeholders. The teachers who instruct in this discipline are important stakeholders and should therefore therefore be integral parts of the planning process for Vocational and Technical Education Programmes. The students for whom the programmes are designed should also play a significant role in influencing the planning process.

Planning for Vocational and Technical Education Programmes must take into consideration the students' need for a particular programmes, employment or higher educational opportunities on completion of High School, availability of a variety of resources (human and material), as well as teachers', students', and community perceptions (Finch & McGough, 1982).

According to a case study on the policy, planning and management of Vocational and Technical Education published by UNESCO, 1984, sound structures, properly coordinated, are of fundamental importance if appropriate policies for Vocational and Technical Education are to be set and, above all, implemented through sound planning and management (UNESCO Document, 1984). The case study also reveals that of the cases presented by the sixteen countries, the matter of Vocational and Technical Education comes under the auspices of Central Government and run by an Education Ministry. Sudan and Turkey are two such countries.

Jamaica is no exception, where a government ministry, such as the Ministry of Education Youth and Culture, is responsible for Vocational and Technical Education, and is responsible for formulating policies to fulfill the mandate of the government. Education at the Secondary level must be responsive to social as well as manpower demands. Vocational and Technical Education is the answer of the Educational system in response to the wide business and their application to society's needs.

Therefore as time passes, policies are adapted to current demands. For example, the government's policy of 1900 – 1960 focused, on, among other areas, the establishment of Vocational and Technical institutions designed to provide the manpower requirement for the economic development of the country, to inculcate social attitudes considered necessary for the social development of the population (Ministry of Education Technical and Vocational Unit, 2002).

The effectiveness of any programme, is determined by the extent to which the curriculum planning process is carried out. According to Finch and Crunkilton, (1999), schools must assume the responsibility to develop, plan, and implement curricula that meet the needs of both students and society. Good curriculum planning incorporates sound decision making policies, set standards for decision making as well as the identifying of needed data such as students' interests, future enrollments, facilities, identifying resources and community participation, to name a few.

In keeping with Site-based and School-based Management, those who work in a local school system, given their skills, and years of experience, are best suited, to provide input to sound decision-making. It also includes development of vision and mission statements, participation from stakeholders, set realistic goals, formulate action plans, identify resources, and monitor and evaluate progress. Velde et al (1999) assert that school personnel and employers must work together to ensure that the curriculum meets the needs of both students and employers.

METHODOLOGY

This research seeks to determine the perceptions of Teachers and Students about the planning of Vocational and Technical Educations in High Schools. In doing so answers were sought for the following questions:

1. What are the perceptions of students regarding the planning of Vocational and Technical Education Programmes in their schools?

2. What are the perceptions of teachers regarding the planning of Vocational and Technical Education Programmes in their schools?

Two 36-item questionnaires, comprising of closed-response items were developed, one for the teachers and one for the students. Such instruments according to Finch and Crunkilton (1999), work well with students and instructors alike, since they may each have different views. The questionnaires were piloted and revised before their administration on the sample. The data collected were descriptively analyzed, looking at the frequencies and percentages of the responses.

The sample size of the study is 374, comprising of 58 Vocational and Technical Education teachers and 316 Grade 11 students, purposefully selected from four Jamaican High Schools. Students shared their perceptions about the planning of Vocational and Technical Education Programmes in their schools.

DATA ANALYSIS AND DISCUSSION OF RESULTS

Table 1 provides data about students' perceptions of the planning of Vocational and Technical Education Programmes in their schools.

Table 1: Students' Perceptions of the Planning of Vocational and Technical Courses

Item #	Summary of Items	SA		A		U		D		SD		Total	
		F.	%	F	%	F.	%	F.	%	F.	%	F	%
19	Need for more hands-on approach	76	24	145	45.9	53	16.8	24	7.6	18	5.7	316	100
20	Counselling provided for selection of courses.	41	13	99	31.3	76	24	77	24.4	23	7.3	316	100
21	No preparation for job interviews.	26	8	81	26	54	17	91	29	64	20	316	100
22	Irrelevant Vocational Courses.	29	9	76	24	34	11	103	33	74	23	316	100
23	Job experience should be included in the course.	200	63.3	89	28.2	12	3.8	7	2.2	8	2.5	316	100
Total		372	117.3	490	155.4	229	72.6	302	96.2	187	58.5	1580	500

n = 316

Most of the students in the sample (69.9%) agreed (strongly agreed and agreed) that there should be more hands-on approach in the delivery of the Vocational and Technical Education Programmes. Some students, (13.3%) disagreed. Only 44.3% of the students agreed (strongly agreed and agreed) that counseling was provided for them in the choice of their courses, while 31.7% of them disagreed that this actually happened. As many as 24% of the students were undecided in their responses.

Some of the students, (49%) disagreed that students were not prepared for job interviews, while 34% of them agreed that no preparation for job interviews took place. There were students (56%) who disagreed that the Vocational and Technical Course offerings were irrelevant; while a smaller percentage (33%) agreed that the courses were in fact irrelevant to the immediate needs of the society. Most of the students (91.5%) agreed that the opportunity to do job experience programmes should be included in the course. A small number of them, (4.7%), however, disagreed.

Table 2 on the next page, provides data about teachers' perceptions of the planning of Vocational and Technical Education Programmes in selected High Schools.

As shown in Table 2, many teachers (60%) agreed (Strongly Agreed and Agreed) that the planning of Vocational and Technical Education Programmes should be undertaken by teachers. Only 31% disagreed. All teachers, (100%) also disagreed that only the less brilliant students should be taught Vocational and Technical Education Courses.

At the same time most of them, 95% felt that there needed to be more community involvement in the planning of the programme. There was also a general consensus among some teachers (88%) that more long term planning should be done. Some teachers (70%) also agreed (Strongly Agreed and Agreed) that the class sizes were too large. Twenty-nine (29%) of the teachers were either undecided or disagreed that the class sizes were too large.

Table 2: Teachers' Perceptions of the Planning of Vocational and Technical Education Programmes in High Schools.

Item #	Summary of Items	SA		A		U		D		SD		Total	
		F	%	F	%	F	%	F	%	F	%	F	%
7	Planning of Tec/Voc to be done by teachers	14	24	21	36	5	9	13	22	5	9	58	100
8	Only less brilliant students to be taught Tec/Voc.	0	0	0	0	0	0	11	19	47	81	58	100
9	More community involvement needed	34	59	21	36	3	5	0	0	0	0	58	100
10	More long term planning needed	18	31	33	57	4	7	2	3	1	2	58	100
11	Too large class sizes	23	40	18	31	5	9	12	20	0	0	58	100
	Total	89	154	93	160	17	30	38	64	53	92	290	500

n = 58

DISCUSSION OF RESULTS

Vocational and Technical Education subjects are practically oriented and therefore must provide students with the opportunity to physically interact with equipment and other materials. This hands-on approach, which students said was lacking or limited, serves the purpose of putting theory into practice, thus strengthening the application of concepts. This would require more equipment, smaller class sizes and more physical space.

It should be understood therefore, that effective planning would take all such factors into consideration. Many students are not sure what subjects they should pursue and therefore the process of counseling should greatly assist students in making the right choices of Vocational and Technical Courses.

It is of concern that 31.7% of the students disagreed that counseling was provided and 24% of them were undecided as to whether or not it was done. This leads me to believe that the counseling that is done for selection of Vocational and Technical Education courses needs to be more effective. Since most business places conduct interviews for prospective workers, it is important that schools prepare students for such an experience. The fact that so many students were either in agreement (34%) or undecided (17%) was not very convincing that adequate preparation was done to help these Grade 11 students to sit interviews.

Most students (91.5%), as shown above, felt strongly that the programme should be so planned so that work experience opportunities are included in the Vocational and Technical Education Courses at every level. Job experience is a way of exposing and orienting students to the real world of work. It is also essential that the courses that they do in school are relevant to the needs of the society. There were a few students who felt that some subjects were irrelevant.

With regards to the planning of Vocational and Technical Education Programmes therefore, many students perceived that not only there was a need for a more hands-on approach to the teaching of Vocational and Technical Courses, but also that there should be an opportunity to have an experience of the world of work by participating in Job experience programmes. Based on students' responses, there are weaknesses in the quality of Vocational guidance as well as in the preparation to do interviews.

Planning for Vocational and Technical Education should also take into consideration, structure their planning keeping in focus the needs of society and ensure that students can in fact obtain jobs, even on a small scale on leaving school.

Teachers are also important stakeholders, who are responsible for disseminating information to their students and to ensure that the goals and objectives of the institution are met. Their training and experience have provided teachers with the confidence and expertise needed to be involved in the planning of Vocational and Technical Education Programmes. Their close interaction with students enable them not only to understand students' capacity to learn, but also to provide activities of interest to them and skills which are needed both for further studies and for the job market.

There is also a general feeling that Vocational and Technical subjects should be taught to all students regardless of their academic abilities. Society needs competent and brilliant persons who can apply their knowledge to provide a competent workforce. Many jobs are poorly done because academic competence and Vocational aptitude are not allowed to come together.

There is also a need for more community participation in the planning of Vocational and Technical Education Programmes. According to Finch and Crunkilton (1999), the involvement of parents, business, industry, and the public through meaningful partnerships will help create an educational programme that will not only serve the students, but also the community in which the school is located.

There are varieties of ways by which this can be done. These include input from retired tradesperson, skilled crafts persons, employers who provide job experiences for students, Parent Teachers' Associations, Advisory Committees. One should also bear in mind that in each community there are vast supplies of resources which if tapped, can greatly enhance the Vocational and Technical Education Programmes in the schools.

A major concern of the Vocational and Technical Education Programme is not only the provision of adequate curriculum materials, but also the continuous expenditure demanded. Much of the monies allocated to the Department are used to furnish equipment, supplies, and tools needed for laboratory instruction. It is virtually impossible to purchase all the curriculum materials necessary at any given time to satisfy the needs of the programme, and therefore long term plans must be made to purchase them.

Teachers were not happy with the large classes and rightly so since given the practical nature of Vocational and Technical Education, more careful attention must be given to students, and also the provision of adequate tools and equipment would for the large numbers at any one time would be difficult, if not virtually impossible.

FINDINGS AND IMPLICATIONS

The following were the major findings and implications of the study:

1.   One hundred percent (100%) of the teachers were in agreement that they should play a leading role in the Planning of Vocational and Technical Education Programmes, apparently because they had the expert knowledge by way of training and experience. There was a general agreement by principals, teachers and the students themselves that the major stake holders – teachers, students, and the community should be involved in the planning of Vocational and Technical Education Programmes.

2.   There was a general agreement, as expressed by 100% of the teachers, contrary to the views of many, that not only less brilliant students should do Vocational and Technical Education Courses, but all students should be equally exposed to this discipline.

3.   Students of varying abilities are entered for Vocational and Technical Education Programmes, and their socio-economic statuses were not determining factors. Students who pursue Vocational and Technical Education Courses were beginning to gain respect on par with those who pursued Academic courses. This fulfills one of the objectives of the Ministry of Education Youth and Culture (MOEYC) which aims at ending the age-old practice of relegating to the trades(workshops), those students who are ill prepared to enter the academic stream (Technical & Vocational Unit, Ministry of Education & Culture)

4.   If teachers are allowed to participate in the planning of Vocational and Technical Education Programmes, these programmes will benefit from their knowledge and experiences of the day-to-day challenges. Finch and Crunkilton (1999) postulate that representatives from those who will be teaching the curriculum content and using the materials, should also be included when preliminary planning is taking place.

5.   If all High School students are exposed to Vocational and Technical Education Programmes as much as they are exposed to academic subjects, the practice of ability streaming would discontinue.

CONCLUSIONS

Arising from the data analysis I have concluded that planning for Vocational and Technical Education Programmes in the High Schools needs closer collaboration between the major stakeholders, such as Teachers, Students, and the community, in addition to the policy makers. Not only would it enrich the Programmes with a wide range of ideas, but it would position the school to obtain human and financial assistance from the school environment.

The parents themselves could be called upon to make contributions. Although teachers in those schools are displaying good performances, with additional help to what the Ministry of Education is doing much more could be achieved.

There is also a need in the High Schools for the pupil/teacher ratio to be reduced for the proper management of the Vocational and Technical Programmes. These practically oriented Programmes require much individual attention, and as reflected in the findings above, the classes are too large. Finally, the recognition of teachers and students perceptions will go a far way in improving the quality of instruction, and planning in Vocational and Technical Education Programmes.

REFERENCES

Bastick, T. & Ezenne, A (2003). Teaching Caribbean Students – Research on Social Issues in the Caribbean and Abroad, Kingston: U.W.I Jamaica: Department of Educational Studies.

Finch, C. R. & Crunkilton, J. (1999). Curriculum Development in Vocational and Technical Education, Library of Congress Cataloguing-in-Publication data, Virginia: Allyn & Bacon.

Finch C. & McGough, R. (1982). Administering and Supervising Occupational Education, Englewood Cliffs, New Jersey: Prentice Hall, Inc.

Ministry of Education Youth and Culture (1996). Rationalization of Technical and Vocational Education and Training (TVET) in the Secondary System, Technical and Vocational Education Unit, Kingston: Ministry of Education, Youth and Culture.

Ministry of Education, Youth and Culture (2002). Technical and Vocational Education Unit (TVU), Kingston: Pear Tree Press Ltd.

Mitchell, P. (1999). Education Journey into the future, Budget Presentation, Ministry of Education, Kingston: Planning Institute of Jamaica, (PIOJ).

Musaazi, J. C. S. (1982). The Theory and Practice of Educational Administration. London and Basingstoke: Macmillan Publishers Ltd.

UNESCO (1984). Policy, planning and Management in Technical and Vocational Education, A comparative Study, Paris: 7 place de Fontenoy, 75700.

Velde, C. J., Cooper, T., Harrington, S., & Mailer, E. (1999). Vocational Educators' Perspectives of Workplace Learning: A Case Study on Senior Schooling; Journal of Vocational Education and Training, Volume 51, Number 1, 1999.

White Paper on Education, the Way Upward (2001). Kingston: Ministry of Education, Youth and Culture.

EARL CHRISTIAN & AUSTIN EZENNE

Chapter 10

CHARTING THE EDUCATION
TRANSFORMATION PATH:
TOWARDS MODELS OF PRAXIS
FOR TEACHER DEVELOPMENT
FOR SCHOOL IMPROVEMENT IN
JAMAICA

PAULETTE FERARIA

ABSTRACT

This article examines the school as the axis and centre of education change processes and explores the change processes that teachers must engage in to close the transformation gap and access the transformation path that leads to a dynamic education system in which change is a process for achieving goals and is sustained as the impetus that constantly engenders alternatives and nurtures efficacy, efficiency and relevance.

Three strategies, shaped by the impetus that 'education is everybody's business' are envisaged as instigators of the change processes: teacher appraisal and development as a coordinating strategy for school improvement; the Bachelor in Education school-based teaching practicum as a collaborative strategy for teacher development and school improvement; and school and community 'business' projects for social reform and sustainability. These strategies guide the six models of teacher development designed by the writer, that schools can adopt /adapt to empower teachers as initiators of school development and improvement: Educating Teachers as Reflective Practitioners; Teacher self-directed and Self-initiated Learning; Peer Observation, Appraisal and Coaching; Staff Professional Development and Training; Teacher Intervention, Innovation and Experiment in Teaching; and Classroom Research and Publication.

Findings from current research in the implementation of aspects of these models are indicating that the path to transforming education in Jamaica must begin with teachers revisiting teaching, re-educating the self and re-positioning the teacher- self as an agent of change. The new and emerging roles of teachers as investigators and researchers, innovators of the teaching experience and quality control and intervention consultants are indicating that new dispositions towards school management must be embraced and guided by the philosophy that leadership that empowers others is central to success, especially in relation to decision-making.

INTRODUCTION

The recently commissioned Task Force on Educational Reform in Jamaica (2004)reported on various anomalies that impede education transformation in the 'current path" that our nation Jamaica is traveling. Despite high levels of enrollment, significant curriculum reform and other efforts such as on-going in-service teacher training, performance targets at all levels of the education system are well below the targets set out in curricula goals and Ministry of Education papers tabled in Parliament. The education system does not provide incentives for principals and teachers to produce greater achievement, nor does it hold them accountable. The commissioned Task Force revealed yet another gap between what we plan to do and what we actually practice and this is, despite the thrust of the Public Sector Modernization Vision and Strategy 2002-2012 to introduce performance management and the attendant pay based on performance which some perceive would no doubt raise levels of teacher performance and improve the effectiveness and efficiency of our education product, teachers continue to be paid through automatic salary increases and increments based on the acquisition of additional qualifications. While remuneration is a key factor in job satisfaction one cannot underestimate the satisfaction that success brings. But the findings from investigations carried out by the Task Force are pointing to teacher incompetence and ineffective management as contributory factors to the transformation gap.

The questions that these observations now raise is- Who will close these gaps? How will these gaps be closed? The answer seems to lie in the paradox of praxis. The custodians of the current path on which the education is traveling must close the transformation gap that leads to the transformation path. But how can the custodians make this leap when they are also the gatekeepers of the institutionalized practices that perpetuate the fossilization of inefficiency and ineffectiveness that have nurtured failure?

THE PURPOSE AND OBJECTIVES OF THE PAPER

This article is intended to open the debate that custodians of education must all engage in if we are to think seriously about charting the educational path into new terrains that will not only close gaps in the short –term short-lived manner likened unto the approach and methods we use to treat potholes and large gaps in our Jamaican parochial roads but open highways for mastery, efficiency, efficacy and sustainability in our educational administration and practices. This article will initiate discussions as follows:

(i) explore the roles of teachers as agents of change, the facilitators of school improvement and the trail blazers of the path that will transform schools and reform education;

(ii) present the synopsis of six models of praxis that could foster teacher appraisal as a coordinating strategy in establishing a culture of appraisal and development that empowers teachers as agents of change; and

(iii) propose the school-based B. Ed practicum as the ideal context for continuous teacher authentication that is initiated by teacher appraisal and development through collaborative (school, community college and university)and sustainable practices.

BACKGROUND

THE TRANSFORMATION GAP

INSTITUTIONALIZED UNDERACHIEVEMENT: A COLONIAL LEGACY?

Ranson (1992), referring in particular to the education culture in Britain, argues that the cause of underachievement lies in the long cultural tradition of educating a minority (not the Minorities, my emphasis). Only a few succeeded because that is what the society had preferred. He further suggests that an analysis of the dominant characteristics of the educational and political systems reveals that underachievement has been institutionalized. Should the current state underachievement in our students' academic performance, our performance targets, teaching outputs and the overall low performance in all areas of the Jamaican education system be now viewed as part of the legacy of British colonial rule? If we were to accept this view, then we would in fact be acknowledging and accepting that the philosophical principles that determine the organizing principles of the Jamaican education system have created a system that paradoxically can be more accurately described as a system of failure rather than of enabling, recording and celebrating achievement because the system has been designed primarily for the purposes of differentiation and selection. The investigators on the Task Force on Educational reform in Jamaica reported that there were enough indicators to conclude that the entire system is performing poorly and urged the nation to see this as a key issue that necessitates the call for accountability for performance at all levels.

THE PROFESSIONAL AND MANAGEMENT GAPS IN EDUCATIONAL PRACTICE

Researchers have always referred to the gap which exists between theory (what is taught in college) and practice (what goes on in classrooms). Evans (1997) cites the difficulties faced by teachers in making the transition from college to the classroom. The research indicates that while there are problems which have to do with the administrative practices of the school, of major significance are the difficulties faced by the teacher in using the knowledge acquired in their training. These findings echo the observation that within the teaching profession, there seems to be an insurmountable gap between theory and practice. The professional gap is sustained and widened by the paradox of teaching which is balancing a teaching theory that is aimed at discovering "truth" with practice which is aimed at bringing about change. While we are able then to identify these gaps we have not successfully implemented the 'fillings' that bring about change,

It is not unusual for teachers to view change as 'a matter for the administration and the 'ministry' and so the idea of the 'teacher as a change agent' is perceived in the realm of 'theory ' to be put into practice by 'management' and is not conceptualized as a salient part of the disposition of the teacher. Teachers who share this view are absolving themselves and have placed accountability in the hands of the principal and managers of school. Teachers who display these attitudes would not necessarily view themselves as part of the management team in schools. Current practices do not socialize the stakeholders in education to be viewed in this manner.

The investigators also reported that there are gaps at different managerial levels in the system. In general, the central Ministry of Education and Youth and the regional offices have a weak management information culture that militates against setting targets and ensuring accountability. The researchers cite the KPMG report and note that there are a number of teachers who are unable to perform adequately, lacking capability, motivation and commitment to professional standards and that principals do not possess the managerial skills or are often ill-prepared for their leadership responsibilities. This is compounded by the fact that the principal does not have the autonomy to obliterate the constraints of institutionalized factors related to staffing and supervision. These gaps in leadership, management and practice underscore that there is a reigning culture of lack of expertise in teaching and the management of teaching.

TRANSFORMING THE JAMAICAN EDUCATIONAL LANDSCAPE

TRANSFORMATION AND CHANGE IN THE MANAGEMENT OF TEACHER EDUCATION

The legacies of colonialism that are sustained in current educational practices challenge us to approach the concept of change within Caribbean contexts in revisionist agendas that call for the educating of our people to discover worth in our environment and then to work for and with others in developing and sustaining what is valuable and meaningful. (Wilson & Morrissey,1995). In this light critical reflexive praxis is applied to education and other sectors to re-align, reform and redress those practices that have marginalized us because of our unique experience and needs. There is an urgent need for localized models and portraits of expertise for viability.

Teacher professional education and training should be centered on enhancing the professional's ability for reflection –in- action and developing the ability for continued learning and problem solving throughout the professional's career. As a reflective practitioner, the teacher has the ability to close the gap between theory and practice, between college and university knowledge and classroom practice. Reflective practice is important as it questions the types and quality of information teachers use in the planning of their professional actions. Moreover it suggests the presence of other and more relevant and valid sources of knowledge and information that is available and if harnessed will facilitate improvement of professional competence.

There is a growing body of literature that is clarifying the procedures and strategies that educators believe contribute successfully to developing the character of the reflective practitioner. Within the literature are emerging themes that provide insights for college as well as university programmes and courses in teacher training and teacher development. There is much talk about educational reform and teachers as agents of school reform. But teachers can only fulfill these roles if they are empowered to do so. Cochran- Smith (1991) describes the preoccupation with reforming classroom practice as *teaching against the grain* and notes the potency of *critical dissonance* – the critical attitude among teachers that leads to the questioning and challenging of theories and policies about classroom practice. Educational programmes which aim at developing critical dissonance, must have the mechanisms in place that will foster teachers' analytical skills and cultivate the disposition to question their own assumptions through reflection on practice. This is the beginning process for transforming and reforming teachers, tutors, and everyday classroom life. Reflective practice fosters *change from within* that is activated by an internal self dialogue. Thus this act of *teaching against the grain* has the potential to be controversial as it challenges or contradicts what has become acceptable and not necessarily workable in our educational practices.

CHANGING SCHOOLS: LEARNING TO TRANSFORM LEARNING IN PRIMARY AND SECONDARY SCHOOLS

There is an urgent need for fundamental change in schools. There is a need for reforms that will not allow educators to perpetuate the mistakes of the past and to enable them to prepare more adequately for the future. The overall aim for all schools involved in change processes is to achieve quality development. Quality development is engendered by three purposes. These are *proving, improving* and *learning.* The principal, teachers and students are all engaged in learning school: proving by fulfilling accountability requirements; improving learning and teaching and learning to support teachers as learners and schools as learning communities. The priority of the nation must be both to change the purposes of education and to embody in the reform of social and political institutions, the organizing principle of learning.

In the Jamaican context, learning starts first with the long term process of transforming the way people think about themselves and what they are capable of and shaping our methods of implementation accordingly. Valuing the dignity and identity of each person to develop the self esteem is a precondition for learning. One of the dispositions that educational transformation should nurture is, "Education is an attitude." Schools must nurture the belief in individual capacity and achievement and this must be the basis of expectation of all learners. To learn is to reach out. Outward-looking education fosters active citizenship.

CHANGING TEACHERS: THE TEACHER-SELF AS AGENT OF CHANGE

Change is a personal and complex phenomenon. Teachers need time in order to reflect, examine, expand and reshape their beliefs and it takes an even longer time to dismantle cherished assumptions and practices and reconstruct and replace with alternative ways of knowing and doing. If change is viewed as development in use then new dispositions towards teaching and learning will take two to three years, not a term! The key to successful change is to find ways of increasing teachers' acceptance of innovation so that they incorporate them in what they do in their classrooms daily. The focus would then shift from teacher behaviour but on the effects their teaching has on learners

Before the teacher can make the leap to assume the role as change agent, he or she has to first think of *the self* as an integral part of his or her being and the *teacher self* that he or learns *to be* in the process of enacting the curriculum.

Chavez (1997) investigated the enactment of three curricular constructs that are salient for curriculum delivery. These are the construct *to be* which is teachers' self authentication (learning to be); the construct *to know* which is the ability to generate knowledge from one's own interpretation of what practice should be and the reflection on and development of that practice; and the construct *to know how to do the right thing* which is developing and perfecting practice, the interpretation and implementation of curricular objectives and approaches. These constructions are pivotal to in curriculum enactment but they also form the basis for engendering the *teacher self* that must be understood by the teacher if he or she is to engender the self as an agent of change.

Once these constructs are harnessed, the next step would be to make the shift from the spectator role of watching and waiting to see how the 'right people' change the situation towards being engaged in personal development and active participant within the school and the wider community. This personal development embraces self development for autonomy, choice, responsibility and accountability. This shifting of stances and dispositions are best activated in activities that engage the teacher in revisiting teaching.

THE B. ED PRACTICUM: CLOSING GAPS, CHARTING NEW PATHS IN TEACHING

The practicum component of the Bachelor in Education degree and the particular re-visit to teaching

280

that it affords, provides the opportunity for practitioners and professionals to begin to address professional gaps through the type of critical inquiry into practice that will initiate the consciousness–raising that facilitates the re-shaping of character which is paramount in the empowerment of teachers to become the chief instigators in education change processes. This global trend in current approaches to school-based work converge on some thematic concerns that now emerge from the literature as well as from empirical research carried out in practicum settings. More and more researchers are collecting data from actual classroom practice that privilege the roles of teachers as observers, recorders, researchers and reporters. (Feraria,2000,2004) This re-visit facilitates the type of teacher empowerment which generates from a revision of the roles related to one's practice. Role revision then becomes the catalyst for the changes teachers will inevitably make to their practice. Some of the dominant themes that generate from such empowered stances are:

- intuitive practice and the power of self-interrogation that leads to dismantling cherished assumptions and narrow views
- intervention as a strategy for closing gaps in Fostering the teacher's role as researcher and exploring one's view of teaching through writing
- Conscious recall and examination of the experience of teaching as a basis for evaluation and classroom teaching as a catalyst for planning and action

- Improving the quality of teaching and student learning through experiment, innovation and intervention (Feraria, 2000; 2004)

These new dispositions towards teaching have been observed in the classroom practice, diaries and logs of teachers of English engaged in the B.Ed practicum in new teaching-learning settings as part of the fulfillment for the Bachelors in Education. These are value-added experiences allowed teachers to develop and nurture dispositions that engender appraisal, advocacy and proactive school practices that initiated transformation in the way they viewed themselves, their students,teaching and schooling.

TRANSFORMING THE SCHOOL CULTURE: MODELS OF PRAXIS

This article proposes the following six models of praxis that were designed by the writer who worked as lecturer and supervisor in BEd practicum settings with teachers of English and teachers in other disciplines. These models of praxis are likely to inject and sustain a school culture of performance and appraisal that embraces the processes of *reflection –on –action, reflection –in –action* and *reflection- for action* in which appraisal is channeled towards teacher-self directed learning that has the potential to generate the process of a whole-school review as a significant aspect of a more comprehensive appraisal strategy that leads to greater accountability in the management of schools. Secondly, the Bachelor in Education school-based practicum can be harnessed as a professional development activity not only for teachers pursuing the degree but for cooperating teachers and other staff members whose strengthens and weaknesses are identified in the appraisal process and incorporated in different roles and functions in the collaborative exercise that the practicum offers for teacher development and further inquiry and research that provide insights for school improvement. These models also provide the opportunity for stakeholders to collaborate in school, home and community-based projects making education everybody's business.

MODEL 1- EDUCATING TEACHERS AS REFLECTIVE PRACTITIONERS (ETRP)

There is a growing body of literature that is clarifying the procedures and strategies that educators believe contribute successfully to developing teachers as reflective practitioners thus re-shaping the character of the practicing teacher. While this can be achieved through professional education and development programmes such as the current Bachelor in Education being offered by the Department of Educational Studies, University of the West Indies, (Mona) the sustainability of continuous self assessment and self report through reflection on practice and investigation of teaching as a catalyst for planning and action are guaranteed in school-based settings where these practices are linked to teacher appraisal and school improvement and development.

The practicum model provides the opportunity for universities/ colleges and schools to involve new stakeholders in the training and education of teachers. The cooperating teachers in practicum schools must be groomed for new roles as mentors, joint-planners, co-innovators and observers of the teaching experience as engaging in these activities would initiate the reflective stances that foster professional development on the job.

MODEL 2: TEACHER SELF-DIRECTED AND SELF—INITIATED LEARNING (TSL)

Teachers are highly motivated when they create their own learning goals based on personal assessment of their needs. Such disposition towards learning and professional development is well represented in the literature on adult learning. Teacher self –dialogue or self-interrogation is the first step towards teacher - change practices. Learning, in this sense, is about reflection –in-action. It involves questioning the way we teach and the assumptions we make about learners and learning. This leads to action-oriented classroom investigation and research and continuous or on-going reflection and self –evaluation. These practices initiate the classroom and school ethos that foster on- going appraisal and action.

The best performance and evaluation practices are those that enable teachers to develop *reflective experimental practice.* Reflecting on and experimenting with practice help teachers to make principled decisions. It is about developing teachers' self-knowledge, the ability to see through teaching situations and understanding the meaning of what is happening in their classrooms and schools. Reflection on practice is not just about learning from experience in a private and solitary way, it is about the production of knowledge about, self, learners, learning and teaching that enlighten and empower teachers. When teachers are engaged in the process of reflection that leads to empowerment, they become proactive about their practice and constantly acknowledge that it can always be improved in some way.

MODEL 3- PEER OBSERVATION APPRAISAL AND COACHING (POAC)

While the teacher is responsible for investigating his/her needs and turning these needs into goals, this practice can be further strengthened by peer observation and coaching. Teachers should be able to investigate the classroom of their peers to collect data on teaching and learning that can be later reflected on and analyzed. These are practices that take place over a period of time and the sustained reflection -on -action has the potential to give teachers a framework within which they can take charge of their own development with the intention of improving the quality of teaching and learning.

In peer coaching, colleagues observe and coach each other using a defined protocol as guideline. The aim is to inform practice for the purpose of improving student learning. Peer coaching can be useful when colleagues use it to refine instructional practices; implement a new instructional strategy; or to solve problems in classroom management, instruction and assessment. (Carr, Herman and Harris,2005)

MODEL 4: PROFESSIONAL DEVELOPMENT AND TRAINING (PDT)

The teacher development and training model is the most widely used by the Professional Development Unit (PDU) of the Ministry of Education and Youth in Jamaica and has been identified as the 'treatment' that is given to teachers who fall below standard in the Performance Evaluation Report (PER). An assumption that underlies teacher development through training is that training might include the exploration of theory, demonstrating or modeling and practice of a skill, feedback about performance and on the job coaching that teachers can refer to or apply to improve their practice. One often-neglected aspect of PDT is the teacher's personal theory and pragmatic adaptation and appropriation of approaches and strategies in order to improve teaching. Such teacher specific and contextualized praxis that focus on day –to-day teaching and learning activities at the school level are the kinds of professional development efforts that are engendered by the interrogation of practice in the appraisal process. When PDT coordinates with teacher self-directed learning (TSL) the result is that this leads to the development of teachers in their roles as change-agents in school development and improvement projects.

MODEL 5: TEACHER INTERVENTION, INNOVATION AND EXPERIMENT IN SCHOOL DEVELOPMENT AND IMPROVEMENT PROJECTS (TIESDIP)

Appraisal offers a strategy that enables schools to draw together their development and action plans, to establish priorities and bring about individual and institutional improvement. In this light teachers must be viewed as interventionists in classroom and school practices that militate against quality education and quality schools and innovators and instigators of the solutions. The teacher's own practice and the school's educational goals and practices are held up for scrutiny and teachers and school mangers take ownership of the problems so as to become part of the solution. This can only be achieved when there is a reorientation in the school management culture of looking outward to the Ministry for top-down solutions while ignoring the far-reaching effects of school-based policy and praxis.

MODEL 6: CLASSROOM TEACHER RESEARCH AND PUBLICATION (CTRP)

This sixth model of appraisal –oriented practice reflects the belief that teachers have the ability to formulate valid questions about their own practice and to engage in objective classroom inquiry that seeks answers to these questions. This is a very powerful tool for the professional development of teachers as researchers. This type of development is individual as well as collective as when combined with the publication of research it provides not only answers to practitioners faced with similar inquires but motivates other readers to develop the spirit and discipline of research in their own classrooms.

MODEL IMPLEMENTATION AND THE B.ED PRACTICUM

The school-based practicum provides the opportunity for the collaboration of student teachers and school-based cooperating teachers in the implementation of an experiment, innovation or intervention inspired by any of the foregoing models as well as the emerging possibilities for school-initiated and university endorsed collaboration for teacher authentication and accreditation for teacher re-licensing. The opportunities for reflective practice, classroom intervention, teaching experiments and innovation that are driven by teachers' emerging philosophies shaped by theory and current research and pedagogy make the collaborative B. Ed practicum an appropriate context for the on-going upgrading of in-service teachers' knowledge, skills and disposition towards teaching.

Over the years the Department of Educational Studies,University of the West Indies, Jamaica campus, has engaged practicing teachers pursing the degree in discussions and activities that educate them as reflective practitioners who acquire new dispositions about teaching that distil notions of the practicum as a repetitive exercise that was already done in college and to see this revisit to teaching as value added experience in the career of teaching. The course of actions that teachers now take to the classroom are not prescriptive but are born out their intervention into classroom practices that give students greater access to learning, improve their own practice and implement cutting edge practices that can be added to the cooperating teacher's repertoire.

The practicing teachers work in a variety of ways in response to the needs of the learners and the schools. They work with individual students, small groups with special needs or with the whole class. Some teachers plan and deliver workshops with teachers in the practicum schools, especially in literacy interventions in primary and secondary schools or worked with parents and care givers in Early Child hood Education programmes. These processes engage classroom teachers in developing new roles as consultants, teacher trainers, project implementers and researchers of the teaching-learning process.

A REPORT FROM THE FIELD: COLLABORATION AND MENTORSHIP FOR PROFESSIONAL DEVELOPMENT AND TRAINING

This research was carried out in two urban high schools (one traditional,one upgraded). The sample consisted of 24 students doing their practicum at the B. Ed. Level and 16 participating teachers. In one school the practicum took the form a whole school literacy intervention while the other was a practicum for novice teachers built on school-based mentorship.

The results indicated that using the B.Ed. practicum as a model of appraisal fosters greater collaboration among university, colleges and schools and guarantees a higher quality of pedagogical delivery in teacher training and development. There was evidence of greater co-operation among in-service teachers, co-operating teachers and student teachers and greater level of staff motivation and response towards collaborative school development planning. Based on the feedback from student teachers and cooperating teachers as well as the observed practice of cooperating teachers after the intervention there was evidence to support the fact that professional development was experienced by the student teachers as well as the cooperating teachers.

In the second experimental context, six novice teachers pursuing the Bachelor in Education (90-credit programme)who were doing their first school-based practicum were placed in a school where they were mentored by a member of staff, a trained teacher and graduate of the BEd programme. The mentor was relieved of some of her classes which were given to the novice teachers who worked in pairs. The mentorship programme involved goal setting with the supervisor, mentor and novice teachers. The mentor facilitated in unit and lesson planning, professionalism, classroom management and specially arranged sessions to talk about the strengths and weaknesses in the novice teachers' practices. These were punctuated by visits from the university-based supervisor.

The mentorship programme culminated in a post- practicum session chaired by the supervisor. The novice teachers and mentor spoke repeatedly about their professional growth and development and the greater love and respect they now had for teaching. One other outcome from this experiment that gave credibility to this type of teacher training and development was the action taken by the principal. The cooperating teacher who was the mentor in this programme was redeployed as the school's Resource Teacher and the principal requested that the intervention be done throughout the school in the teaching of English as well as mathematics with the next batch of university students.

In an educational environment where alternative forms of appraisals and teacher authentication are being discussed and encouraged, those that are linked to the BEd practicum will find much relevance as they have the potential to initiate on-the-job professional development that can lead to the staff re-deployment for school development.

CONCLUSION: APPRAISING THE TASK AHEAD

At this time when there is a call for new directions in education that privilege localized management systems (*Task Force for Education 2004*) there is need to expedite school-based teacher appraisal task force (no pun intended) initiatives at the school level. Such organized and special operations to develop school-based praxis of teacher appraisal as a coordinating strategy for teacher empowerment and development, improvement and development of quality education and quality schools can begin to pave the way for building a culture of development and empowerment in schools.

This education transformation path is the carving of new possibilities of *being* that emerge from new makings and become committed to shaping a new enabling and regenerative history.This research has shown that these new makings are a collective, shared enterprise in which the voices of all participants must be heard. A pedagogy nurtured by transformed praxis is essentially rooted in the everyday lives of those who conceptualize it and it works from within to engender change from within. 'Working from within' is pedagogic as well as strategic and as such is twinned also with the notion of 'change from within'. The nuances however are the ways in which these stances articulate with teacher appraisal and development processes that activate "listening to the teacher within". The teacher within is not the voice of conscience but of identity and integrity.

Listening to the teacher within in this transformation path means adopting an appraisal and development methodology which privilege working with the teachers within their natural settings (classrooms). This extends the concept of 'teacher within' towards a disposition in teaching and learning that locates expertise or 'know how' in reasoned and reflective practice that connect with the teacher-self,the other teachers within the discipline and the teacher within our own learners.

This is the kind of with-it-ness that has the possibility to transform practice and transform lives.

Change from within explores the notions of teacher empowerment and development through reflective practice and teacher validation of practice as well as the pedagogic stance of 'teaching against the grain' that is essentially political in its agenda. This act of *teaching against the grain* has the potential to be controversial as it challenges or contradict what has become acceptable and not necessarily workable in our educational practices. This act of teaching is potentially emancipating as in the act of going against the established it engenders the alternative. Within this context the transformation path is constructivist as well as de-constructivist as it is developed by progressive teachers attempting to close the transformation gap by eliminating inefficiency and underachievement in teacher as well as student performance.

REFRENCES

Carr, J. F; Herman N; Harris, D. (2005) Creating Dynamics Schools through Mentoring Coaching and Collaboration. Association for Supervision and Curriculum Development. Alexandria: Virginia.

Cochran-Smith (1991) Learning to Teach Against the Grain. *Harvard Educational Review*. Vol. 6: 279-310

Evans, H.(1997) Making the Transition from College to Classroom: What Knowledge do teachers use and why. Caribbean Journal of Education. Vol. 19:1 April.

Feraria, P. J., (2000) Preparing the Teacher as Reflective Practitioner: Some Emerging Trends in a Professional Training Programme at the University of f the West Indies, Mona. *Journal of Education and Development in the Caribbean*

Feraria, P. J., (2004) Prospero's Course and Caliban's Curse: New Lessons in Teacher Education and Training. *Transforming the Educational Landscape*. Edited by Monica Brown and Clement Lambert. Institute of Education. University of the West Indies, Mona.

Ranson, S., (1992). "Towards the Learning Society". Educational Management and Administration. Vol.20. No.2

Task Force on Educational Reform Jamaica: A Transformed Education System 2004.Report presented to The Most Hon. P.J. Patterson by Dr. Rae Davis, Chairman. September 2004.

NOTES ON CONTRIBUTORS

SUSAN ANDERSON

Dr. Susan Anderson obtained her Ph.D in Educational Psychology from the University of the West Indies, Kingston, Jamaica. She is currently the coordinator of graduate programs in the School of Education, the University of the West Indies, Mona.

BÉATRICE BOUFOY-BASTICK

Beatrice Boufoy-Bastick holds a Master's degree from Sorbonne University, Paris and a Ph.D from the University of the West Indies, Kingston, Jamaica. She is a Post-Graduate of London University and her research interests are in the interaction of culture and second language education, in Language Policies and modern language teaching methodologies. Dr. Boufoy-Bastick has a wide cross-cultural experience in teaching and research in Europe, Australia, Asia, the South Pacific, South America and the Caribbean.

BEVERLEY BRYAN

Dr. Beverley Bryan received her Ph.D in Language Education from the University of London. Beverley Bryan is currently the Director of the School of Education and the Head of the Department of Educational Studies at the University of the West Indies Kingston, Jamaica. She has served as the President of the West Indies Group of University Teachers, (WIGUT).

EARL CHRISTIAN

Earl Christian obtained his B.Ed and M.Ed in Educational Administration from the University of the West Indies Kingston, Jamaica. He was a school principal for many years and currently he is an Education Officer in the Ministry of Education and Culture, Kingston, Jamaica.

LORAINE D. COOK

Loraine Cook holds a Ph.D degree in Educational Psychology from the University of the West Indies, Kingston, Jamaica. Dr. Cook's research interests are on teacher's locus of control and evaluation of online academic programs in education. Currently, she is a lecturer in Educational Psychology and Research Methods at the University of the West Indies, Kingston, Jamaica.

AUSTIN EZENNE

Austin Ezenne received his Ph.D in Educational Administration from the University of Wales, Cardiff, United Kingdom. He taught for over twenty-five years in Nigerian Universities before joining the University of the West Indies. He is a member of the British Society for Research into Higher Education (SRHE), the British Educational Leadership, Management and Administration Society (BELMAS), the Association for Supervision and Curriculum Development (ASCD), the Jamaica Association for Human Resource Development (JATAD) and the American Educational Research Association (AERA).

296

PAULETTE FERARIA

Dr. Feraria obtained her Ph.D in Language Education, from the University of the West Indies, Kingston, Jamaica. She is the Associate Dean in the Faculty of Humanities and Education at the University of the West Indies, Mona.

MYRTLE ELAINE HARRIS

Myrtle Harris obtained her M.Ed in Educational Administration from the University of the West Indies, Kingston, Jamaica. She is currently Librarian for the School of Education Documentation Centre, University of the West Indies, Kingston, Jamaica.

DISRAELI HUTTON

Dr. Hutton obtained his Ph.D. in Higher Educational Administration from Bowling Green State University in Ohio, United States. He worked at various levels of the education system, including Senior Director at HEART/NTA, Jamaica, and lecturer at the University of Technology, Jamaica. He was a consultant to the Education Transformation Team and also acted as Executive Director. At present, Dr. Hutton is a lecturer in the Department of Educational Studies, UWI. His specialization is Educational Administration and Supervision.

ZELLYNNE JENNINGS

Zellynne Jennings has two Masters degrees from Universities in the United Kingdom and a Ph.D from the University of the West Indies, Kingston Jamaica. She has served as the Director of the School of Education and the Head of Educational Studies, University of the West Indies, Mona, and as professor of Education at the University of Guyana and at the University of the West Indies where she is currently serving.

BEVERLEY JOHNSON

Mrs. Beverley Johnson is the Principal of Jericho Primary School, a New Horizon Project School in St. Catherine. She is a Ph.D student in Educational Administration, at the University of the West Indies, Kingston, Jamaica. Her research interests are in the areas of Educational Leadership and Supervision.

MILES ANTHONY IRVING

Miles Irving obtained his Ph.D from the University of California. He is an Assistant Professor in the Department of Educational Psychology and Special Education at Georgia State University, Atlanta, Georgia. Dr. Mile's areas of research span cultural identity and academic achievement of African Americans, Africans and Caribbean University students.

CLAUDETTE PHOENIX

Claudette Phoenix was awarded her Masters degree in Measurement and Evaluation by the University of Guyana. She is currently Head of the Measurement and Evaluation Unit, Ministry of Education Guyana and is responsible for all national examinations in Guyana and for overseeing the assessment components of national projects such as the GoG/IDB Basic Education Access and Management Support (BEAMS) programme. Ms. Phoenix initially joined the staff of the Measurement and Evaluation Unit in 1996 as a Test Development Officer after having served as a classroom teacher at Primary and Secondary Levels for twenty-two years. Her research interests are in developing and evaluating national and regional curriculum based assessments.

Notes

Breinigsville, PA USA
24 May 2010
238610BV00002B/57/P